D0648437

Digital consumers

RESHAPING THE
INFORMATION
PROFESSIONS

Digital consumers

RESHAPING THE
INFORMATION
PROFESSIONS

Edited by

David Nicholas

and Ian Rowlands

facet publishing

Published by Facet Publishing,
7 Ridgmount Street, London WC1E 7AE
www.facetpublishing.co.uk

Facet Publishing is wholly owned by CILIP:
the Chartered Institute of Library and
Information Professionals.

British Library Cataloguing in Publication Data
A catalogue record for this book is available
from the British Library.

ISBN 978-1-85604-651-0

First published 2008

PEFC
PEFC/16-33-111
CATG-PEFC-052
www.pefc.org

Text printed on PEFC accredited
material. The policy of Facet
Publishing is to use papers that are
natural, renewable and recyclable
products, made from wood grown in
sustainable forests. In the
manufacturing process of our books,
and to further our policy, preference is
given to printers that have FSC and
PEFC Chain of Custody certification.
The FSC and/or PEFC logos will
appear on those books where full
certification has been granted to the
printer concerned.

Typeset from editors' disks in 10/15 pt
Bergamo and Unitus
by Facet Publishing.
Printed and made in Great Britain by MPG
Books Ltd, Bodmin, Cornwall.

Contents

Acknowledgements

This book is the fruit of eight years' work researching the digital transition and its impacts and implications for publishers, libraries and the consumer world beyond that. During this period the CIBER (Centre for Information Behaviour and the Evaluation of Research) research group at University College London (UCL) has created a powerful social network of researchers who share a common interest in raising the profile of digital consumer research. The network, like the research field itself, is international and interdisciplinary, and it crosses the academic/practitioner boundary. A number of these researchers are contributors to this book but many others have contributed to our thinking, research and publications. In this regard we would particularly like to thank: Professor Iain Stevenson (UCL), Hamid R. Jamali, who helped prepare the manuscript (UCL), Anthony Watkinson (UCL), Professor Carol Tenopir (University of Tennessee), David Brown (British Library), Bill Russell (Emerald Group Publishing), Graham Taylor (Publishers Association) and Mayur Amin (Elsevier).

Thanks also to our fellow contributors who agreed to write their chapters (for a crate of wine!) and who did so splendidly, with speed and alacrity. We would also like to register our gratitude to our funders who provided us with the money to do the research, which feeds directly into this work. In this regard we would like to thank Lorraine Estelle and Balviar Notay (both the Joint

Information Systems Committee – JISC), Michael Jubb (Research Information Network), Martin Richardson (Oxford University Press), Jan Wilkinson (previously British Library, now Manchester University), Rod Cookson (Taylor & Francis) and Michael Mabe (STM Association, previously Elsevier). Finally, we would also like to thank Helen Carley of Facet Publishing for pressing us to write this book, something that was not easy when the Research Assessment Exercise is always on our minds. We really enjoyed it.

David Nicholas and Ian Rowlands

About the contributors

Dr Tom Dobrowolski

Tom is a senior lecturer and Head of Postgraduate Studies at the Institute of Information Science and Book Studies, Warsaw University, the largest Information School in Poland. He is a founder member of the Centre for Information Behaviour and the Evaluation of Research (CIBER) and is one of its leading digital theorists. Research interests largely concern virtual collections and information networks and Tom has written more than a dozen articles with the CIBER team.

Maggie Fieldhouse

Maggie is a lecturer at the School of Library, Archive and Information Studies (SLAIS) at University College London (UCL). Her resesarch interests are management and collection management; these developed from her previous experience as Information Services Manager at the University of Sussex Library. Current concerns are: pedagogical aspects of information literacy and the relationships between digital literacy and information-seeking behaviour.

Professor Barrie Gunter

Barrie is Head of the Department of Media and Communication, University of Leicester, where he is also Director of the Centre for Mass Communication Research. He was previously Professor of Journalism Studies and founder member of the Department of Journalism Studies, University of Sheffield, where he was Director of Research. He has written over 40 books and more than 250 journal papers, book chapters and technical reports on media, marketing and management issues. He is on the editorial boards of *The Journal of Communication, Journal of Broadcasting & Electronic Media, Human Communication Research, Media Psychology, New Media & Society* and *Trends in Communication*. He has won research grants to the value of more than £800k. Currently he is involved in research on blogging and its impact on mainstream news, the impact of new information and communication technologies in higher education, and the future of television.

Paul Huntington

Paul is a senior research fellow with CIBER at UCL. His main field of expertise is the analysis of server transactional log files. As part of a team he has pioneered techniques for the analysis and understanding of transactional log files (deep log analysis) and has been instrumental in the development of concepts and metrics related to user online behaviour. He has worked, as a member of the research team, for eight years on over 20 separate research projects spanning a variety of platforms including the world wide web, digital interactive television, mobile phones and touch screen kiosks that have generated more than a hundred peer-reviewed articles. Previously Paul worked as a researcher at City University, the University of North London and the University of Hertfordshire.

Dr Hamid R. Jamali

Hamid is an Iranian who is a researcher at UCL SLAIS and is a member of the UCL Centre for Publishing and CIBER. He recently graduated with a PhD degree in Library and Information Studies from UCL and has taken up a lecturership at Tarbiat Moallem University in Tehran, Iran. A library and information scientist by background, his research interests cover information behaviour of scholars, use of electronic information resources and bibliometric studies. He has collaborated on the Virtual Scholar research programme run by CIBER.

Professor Michael Moss

Michael is a research professor in archival studies in the Humanities Advanced Technology and Information Institute at the University of Glasgow. He is a member of the board of the National Trust for Scotland, a non-executive director of The National Archives of Scotland and a member of the Lord Chancellor's Advisory Council on National Records and Archives. His recent publications include 'Choreographed encounter – the archive and public history', *Archives*, vol. xxxii, no. 116, 41–57, 2007; with Alistair Tough as editors, *Record Keeping in a Hybrid Environment: managing the creation, use and disposal of unpublished information objects in context*, Chandos Press, 2006; and with Laurence Brockliss et al. as editors, *Advancing with the Army: medicine, the professions and social mobility in the British Isles 1790–1850*, Oxford University Press, 2006.

Professor David Nicholas

David is the Director of UCL SLAIS. He is also the Director of the UCL Centre for Publishing and a Director of the CIBER research group. He is a member of the British Library Research Board and editor of *Aslib Proceedings*. Research interests largely concern the Virtual Scholar, about which he has published more than a hundred peer-reviewed articles. He has been the principal investigator on nearly 30 projects totalling more than £1,500,000 in value and is currently engaged in investigations of: usage statistics (US Institute of Museums and Library Services), the use and impact of e-journals (for the Research Information Network) and e-books (for the Joint Information Systems Committee – JISC), and open access publishing (for OUP).

Dr Ian Rowlands

Ian is Reader in Publishing at UCL SLAIS and an active member of the UCL Centre for Publishing and CIBER. An information scientist by background, he has maintained a steady interest in the policy aspects of libraries, publishing and new technology for 20 years, working in a variety of settings including industry, consultancy, policy studies and the academy. He recently led the successful 'Google Generation' project for the British Library and JISC, around which his contribution in this volume is based.

Chris Russell

Chris is a founding Director of eDigitalResearch with responsibility for business development, account management and financial operations. The company was founded in 1999 and was created in response to identifying a niche market as numbers of internet companies were rapidly increasing with little appreciation of usability and customer experience issues. Chris has a business degree from Kingston University, and on graduating, he moved into sales and marketing for Smiths Foods and British American Tobacco and later formed his own company in 1986. He has worked for numerous blue-chip companies, including B&Q, BT, thetrainline.com and Comet. These commissions have given him a unique view of the UK digital consumer and the e-shopper in particular. Chris is also a member of CIBER, a Senior Visiting Fellow at UCL and helped to design the Digital Consumers course, which is taught to UCL students.

Peter Williams

Following a successful teaching career which took him to Egypt, Spain and Brazil, Peter has spent the last 12 years investigating the use of ICT applications in the fields of education, health, and the news media. He has worked at City University, the University of East London (UEL), and UCL, where he has returned as research fellow after completing an ESRC-funded project at UEL. This looked at exploiting ICT to help adolescents with learning disabilities with basic skills, communication and self-advocacy. His other work has included evaluating charitable websites designed to help vulnerable youngsters and working with the new media department of a regional newspaper as part of his early research into how journalists were exploiting the internet. He is currently examining how scholars and other eminent people create/acquire, manage and archive digital information. Peter is the lead author of over 40 journal articles and a book.

Richard Withey

Richard has recently stepped down as global director of interactive media for Independent News & Media PLC (INM), a position held since May 2002. He joined INM to set up Independent Digital, the digital publishing arm of Independent News & Media, in June 1999. This followed 12 years at News International, where for seven years he was director of new media, formulating the overall strategy for the successful launch on the web of titles such as *The Times*, *The Sunday Times* and *The Times Educational Supplement*, as well as investing directly or through joint ventures in a number of new media start-ups and publishing ventures. He has wide experience of the digital world having built and sold databases and online retrieval systems in the public and private sectors before joining News International in 1987, including three years as Head of Information Services for the Institute of Management. Until recently he was chairman of the Newspaper Licensing Agency. He is a Fellow of the Royal Society of Arts. Richard holds an Honorary Fellowship at UCL, where he is also a Director of CIBER.

The digital consumer:
an introduction and philosophy

DAVID NICHOLAS
IAN ROWLANDS
RICHARD WITHEY
TOM DOBROWOLSKI

We have chosen the title of this book with care, adopting the more general 'digital consumer' rather than the more specific 'digital information consumer' descriptor in recognition of the fact that, although the book focuses on the behaviour of people visiting the virtual space for information, the internet has redefined and widened the information domain. Because the internet is an encyclopedic, multi-purpose platform that people use, rather like a superstore, to obtain a whole range of things (often at the same time), it is now almost impossible to say what information is and what it is not, what is information seeking and what is not. Being a digital consumer does not simply mean choosing or buying e-documents or information services. Information is also fundamental to the process and success of e-shopping. As Chris Russell in Chapter 3 explains, first a person is a digital information consumer and then an e-buyer. Thus people shopping at the John Lewis e-store will be using the internal search engine to find what they want, navigating through the site employing browsing menus and opening another window on a cross-comparison site to make sure they are getting value for money. It is not surprising therefore that looking for information is one of the two most common web activities – the other is e-mail; the digital consumer is essentially an information consumer. There is another reason for employing the more general form of the descriptor and it is because information seeking is not conducted in a vacuum and many factors shape it. Therefore it is important that it is embedded in a wider world of e-publishing, e-shopping and communication theory.

Why this book now?

Because this book is a first, it fills a yawning gap in our professional knowledge and shows us how we can overcome an insularity that is plainly an obstacle to professional development. Amazingly, despite the fact that we are ten years into an information consumer revolution occasioned by the arrival of the internet, which is changing society, education and commerce on a massive and global scale, this is the first time, as far as we can discover, that information or digital consumers have figured in a book title issued by a publisher providing books for the information professions. Why is this the case when digital consumers worldwide can be numbered in their billions and are rapidly transforming the information landscape through their preference for search engines, dislike of paying for information, and short attention spans? Why is this so when the core information professions – librarianship, archives and records management, publishing and journalism – have been rocked, and, in some instances, derailed, by the digital transition? There are in fact a number of possible explanations, that we shall reflect on throughout this introduction, but the main reason is, probably, that information professions are insular and tribal (something particularly true of librarians) and what happens outside their strictly defined discipline boundaries are not their prime concern, even though the user and internet are busy blowing up and redrawing these boundaries. The once neat demarcation lines that existed between the information professions are becoming obscured as information consumers use their new-found freedom to relocate themselves and their activities in the virtual information space, and take on much of the work previously undertaken by information professionals. This is creating a degree of inter-communal strife, with particularly fierce disputes breaking out between publishers and librarians. These are fiercest in the scholarly communication field, where the introduction of open access and institutional repositories are close to bringing the two communities to blows. E-books, rest assured, are also going to usher in further territorial disputes and skirmishes, with publishers and librarians once again fighting for the spoils, mortally wounding the loser in all possibility.

A second reason is that the digital consumer is now King, and the communication and delivery channels that have opened up are the King's Horses but you would hardly know this from the responses of many information professionals. Indeed, when we first used the term 'consumer' at a conference a few years ago now a number of participants took issue with the term. Their users, customers and clients, which is what they preferred to call them in a misguided attempt to show respect, were not consumers they said, as though this was a form of abuse. It is true that this no longer happens, although people still look rather uncomfortable when we mention the term. But of course in a world where access to information is a key democratic right and leveller, it is not so easy to criticize; political correctness cramps their style. However, the complainants have moved on and there is now a negative reaction when we make comparisons with the e-shopper. Indeed, when it was first mentioned that we would be including a chapter on the e-shopper in this book the reaction could be summarized as 'What the hell does this have to do with libraries, archives, etc.?' Our answer was 'A hell of a lot' as readers of this book will see for themselves, because consumers are now being offered ultimate choice in all aspects of their lives, the effect of which has been rapidly to dismantle the barriers between disciplines, be they professional, social or recreational. Connected consumers now have access, at any time of the day or night, through multiple devices and platforms, to all aspects of their information needs. If the traditional 'gatekeeper' is not there (at best) or gets in the way of this communication (at worst), consumers will abandon them and go their own way. This key aspect of the digital revolution applies to all members of the communication and information food chain, and we ignore it at our peril. There is a real risk of libraries becoming decoupled from the user.

Meeting the needs of a user community increasingly well connected by Facebook, LinkedIn, MySpace and Twitter will not be easy, and it is certainly best approached by thinking about its needs in an entirely different way, which is the kernel of this book. The days of users as supplicants are pretty much over, and thinking about their needs as consumers is a key step-change in delivering the right services. However, few people have confronted the hard truth that their users are no longer in their grip, some have flown away and many new ones have arrived, and the majority of them now use information resources remotely and anonymously. Worryingly, while most people in the information professions are alert to the technical changes that have taken place in the virtual information space, when it comes to users many are going about their business as though nothing really fundamental has happened. Of course, information professionals have been bleating on about 'users' since time immemorial, but they have not really made that much progress in understanding them, certainly not their behaviour at the coal-face. It is almost as if by mentioning the term or having a conference, that this assuages the guilt. Thus, for instance, how many libraries (or publishers for that matter) have a department dedicated to following users' every move and relating that directly to academic outcomes and impacts? How many engage, even at the most basic level, with the kinds of sophisticated market research and demographic profiling that are behind the success of many of the UK's leading retailers or service providers? The answer is, none that we know of, and this is seriously worrying given that to succeed in the information business we need to follow the (anonymous) users' every move; they are after all driving all the major changes in the digital information environment. The big challenge here for us all is in understanding and accommodating the concept of the digital consumer. Failure to do this will result in eventual professional melt-down, the signs of which are already there for all to see.

This then is a book about information users, but not users as we once knew them. They are looking for information, yes, but also for goods, services, new experiences, titillation, excitement and entertainment. These consumers, numbered in their billions, are global 24/7 shoppers. They are the elephant in our room. This is a book for those people that want to believe that what they are doing is relevant to the information age in which we find ourselves, want to be in the fast lane and it is especially for those who lack recognition or long for a sense of purpose or mission.

The third reason why this book is badly needed is because the time has come for all the information professions to re-examine their core values and discipline boundaries, and it has to be said that they have been very slow in doing this. That is why, in an information-rich and information-driven world where there should be plaudits (and not threats) for the information professions, they find themselves challenged and, increasingly, isolated from the main action. The professional responses as determined by information policies, publications and professional education have to be regarded as wholly inadequate. Disintermediation (loosely defined and understood as 'cutting out the middleman'), of course, has left many professionals in a state of shock and denial regarding the benefits that it has delivered – a society in which everyone is waking up to the critical importance of information and finding it. Disintermediation has triggered an information-seeking frenzy on a truly massive scale.

The world has totally changed but we are still relying on belief systems from another age – this is most evident in the information-seeking models we work with. The textbooks and professional tomes produced now are little different than those published five or ten years ago, yet our professions have been turned upside down, inside out. Let us not kid ourselves, the information landscape has been totally transformed. Google now channels millions and millions of people to the information they need, on a scale that dwarfs any library, publishing or newspaper effort. The tail (the retrieval system) is wagging the dog to within an inch of its life.

The prime purpose of this book is to reconnect information workers/providers, from all walks of life, with their user base by putting forward a belief system that will help people understand, engage, relate to each other and survive in a ubiquitous information environment, where information professionals and knowledge providers are no longer the dominant players nor, indeed, the supplier of first choice. Short of appropriate consumer theories, visions and a robust and appropriate evidence base there is a danger that the information professions are becoming increasingly rudderless and estranged from their users and paymasters. The warning signs are already there. Public libraries appear to be in real trouble and academic libraries risk being decoupled from their user base as users continue to flee the physical space. And even the mighty scholarly publishing industry is coming under pressure from the emergence of open access publishing models and institutional repositories.

What is most concerning is that, despite the obvious writing on the wall, too many people are still attempting to defend traditional turf or territory and an obsolete information paradigm. Unfortunately, the majority belong to the library profession. The core realization has to be that the new model for the information/knowledge economy is not being reflected in the institutions that support it, including professional, educational and commercial ones. By widening the information embrace, this book introduces the wider information community to solutions they are seeking, or will be shortly. The book puts forward solutions now for problems that, while only just emerging, are being recognized as potentially cataclysmic for the whole information community.

This book is dedicated to all aspects of information-users-cum-consumers, and it is unique in this respect. Their rapid emergence in the virtual world requires us all to junk much of the intellectual baggage we have acquired over the years regarding use, users and information seeking. This baggage is an impediment to meeting the needs of today's information consumers by means of appropriate and attractive information services. We are lumbered by information-seeking theories and models produced in a hard-copy environment back in the 1980s and 1990s. Do we honestly believe that anything developed then on the back of several dozen people in a particular physical space more than ten years ago has any relevance to what happens today? In this book we blow the whistle on such notions, their time is up.

What makes it even more essential that we learn everything there is to know about the digital consumer is because all their activities take place anonymously in the virtual space and there are a large number of people using digital services information professionals have never encountered before and never will. Therefore, the need to peer into the virtual space, to find out what is going on is so pressing and obvious it is hardly worth saying, except that not enough people do it regularly enough. It is hoped that this book will start people looking by showing what can be seen and how it is best viewed.

The authors and their approach

There are too many authors and conference speakers who peddle visions of a digital future, typically on the basis of no evidence at all. They are the PowerPoint Puff evangelists. This book, despite its novelty, is not in the business of fantasizing; nor is it simply about tomorrow. It is mainly about today because the real problem is not what tomorrow will bring but what today has already brought with it. The beliefs and concepts propounded here in this book are built on a massive evidence base, whether they come from logs, surveys, interviews and focus groups, or the peer-reviewed literature. We do peer into the future at the end of the book but Barrie Gunter does this purely in the context of the research evidence.

The topic demands an interdisciplinary approach for all the reasons previously mentioned and this is provided by a group of authors whose subject strengths between them include psychology (Gunter), media studies (Gunter), journalism (Withey, Gunter and Nicholas), computer science (Dobrowolski and Huntington), information science (Rowlands and Jamali), librarianship (Nicholas, Dobrowolski, Jamali and Fieldhouse), history (Moss), archives (Moss), scholarly communication (Nicholas, Rowlands and Huntington), education (Williams), consumer health (Nicholas, Huntington and Williams), e-commerce (Russell), marketing (Russell) and publishing (Nicholas and Rowlands). The book also hopes to avoid the fragmentation that is so often found in edited, interdisciplinary books, because all the authors know each other, have worked and researched together and respect and understand each other's contribution in the field. All are connected in some way or another to the Centre for Information Behaviour and the Evaluation of Research (CIBER) (www.ucl.ac.uk/slais/research/ciber/) research group that has pioneered digital consumer research. Furthermore, Nicholas, Huntington, Gunter, Withey, Williams and Russell teach on a course called Digital Information Consumers, taught to Information Management undergraduates at University College London (UCL), where many of the ideas presented in this book were developed. Even so, there is diversity and overlap in the offerings of the contributors and this is the inevitable (and welcome) outcome of dealing with a global and fast-changing phenomenon – the like of which has not been witnessed before. Each chapter can be read as a self-contained piece.

Chapters and contributors

Richard Withey sets the stage in Chapter 2, 'The digital information marketplace and its economics: the end of exclusivity'. He provides the essential environmental context for the book by showing how business models that have long supported the information industry are undergoing seismic change, and argues that those who ignore this do so at their peril. He explains that the exclusivity created by the ownership of the printing press is over and that this matters a lot for the information professions. He utilizes his long experience of being a senior executive in the digital information business to make his point with some authority. Chris Russell, one of the country's leading e-commerce analysts, in Chapter 3 'The e-shopper: the growth of the informed purchaser' also provides an essential context for the understanding of the digital consumer. He does this by providing a deep and authoritative insight into the behaviour of digital shoppers and the factors that have shaped their behaviour. E-commerce and e-shopping have led the way and are dominant and pattern-forming activities in the virtual environment and have helped shape the behaviour of the digital information consumer. Usually one and the same person, where the e-shopper goes, the information consumer follows and Chris helps point us to where things are going and what we can expect down the line. For many readers this will represent their first contact with e-shopping concepts and data.

Michael Moss examines the theories that are emerging from all the changes that we are witnessing. He argues that we need to wake up to the realities of the arrival of the second digital revolution that is being colonized by other disciplines with theory and rhetoric that address its far-reaching implications for the way we live and do business. He also argues we should not ignore previous information revolutions, such as the development of printing in 15th-century Europe, and, perhaps more importantly, the long preoccupation with information and its adjuncts in European thought, stretching back to classical times. Barrie Gunter, in Chapter 5 'The psychology of the digital information consumer', provides us with an understanding of human behaviour online. The rules of online interpersonal and human-computer interaction can provide important insights into what lies behind information-seeking behaviour and how to utilize more effectively, and how to design more user-friendly, online communications systems. Psychology rarely figures in the professional literature and this chapter will provide an invaluable introduction to what it can offer to our understanding of the digital information seeker.

At the heart of the book are two research-led chapters on digital information seeking in a virtual environment. The first, 'The information-seeking behaviour of the digital consumer: case study – the virtual scholar' by David Nicholas, Paul Huntington, Hamid R. Jamali and Tom Dobrowolski is the most extensive evaluation of the digital consumer's information-seeking behaviour ever presented. It represents the first airing of CIBER's comprehensive digital information-seeking model, with its 13 individual traits. This is a model that takes cognizance, unlike other models, of the fact that most information seeking in a scholarly environment will soon be virtual. Chapter 6 also discloses the details of the digital footprint that provides the data that populates the model. Chapter 7 by Peter Williams, Ian Rowlands and Maggie Fieldhouse, looks at the information behaviour of young people, commonly referred to as the 'Google Generation', and reviews the available evidence as to whether young people, especially the young scholar, will augur a wholly new way of seeking for information. The thrust of this chapter is that consumer traits conveniently attributed to the young are in fact now mainstream for all ages: it is simply insufficient for information professionals to serve out their time until retirement hoping that it will be someone else's problem. The future is now. In fact the future was five years ago, just nobody noticed. This chapter constitutes the first general release of data from the widely acclaimed Google Generation report (www.ucl.ac.uk/slais/research/ciber/downloads/).

The penultimate chapter sees Barrie Gunter identifying changes in the pipeline that might impact on the digital consumer. He explains that digital information consumers will soon have even more choices to make than ever before in terms of sources of information about commodities and services.

They will also more readily become producers as well as consumers in the digital world with the spread of digital equipment and off-the-shelf tools that enable them to upload their own content online. The rapid evolution of new information and communications technologies will lead to even more shrinkage in the time-lag between innovation launch and reaching a critical mass or 'tipping point' beyond which they spread dramatically from early adopters to the general population.

The final, short chapter is one that we owe to the information community who we all believe have an important and valuable contribution to make in the new information world we are being fast-forwarded to. That is, providing they take on board all that we are saying! To assist in this, we have itemized and prioritized, executive summary style, the essentials.

Intended audience

As mentioned earlier, this book has been published to address widespread concerns being felt by all the information professions – librarians, publishers, journalists and archivists. Of course, many authors will say this in the hope that their sales will receive a boost as a consequence, but we have very good reasons for believing this to be true. The internet has thrown all the individual professions together and they now have much in common and in many cases the user is the same virtual person. However, it is undoubtedly librarians who are currently under the cosh and for them this book should be regarded as an essential survival kit. Because the book sets about the task of changing professional mindsets and because this is easier done with students, who, by definition, should be less set in their ways, we clearly hope that they will read the book in great number and help spread the consumer message.

Knowledge transfer is the current buzz phrase in academe and this book ticks all the right boxes in this respect. We are moving research findings into the practitioner environment, sharing relevant information amongst the information professions. This is the first time these findings have been placed in the professional mainstream and brought together in the form of a professional manual or manifesto.

One final point

You might ask, why have we published these contributions in the form of a book, when they could just as easily have been a 'conversation', a blog, a dialogue, or an online virtual conference? Well, we were asked to, which tells its own story about the readiness of this audience, you, the information professional, to accept change. If this book has one message, it is captured in the words of E. M. Forster: 'Only connect, and the beast and the monk, robbed of the isolation that is life to either, will die. . . . Live in fragments no longer. Only connect.' (Forster, Howards End, 1910).

The web connects. The beasts and the monks are, of course, the information professionals, isolated from what is actually going on. The internet is taking user/consumer connectivity to a new level, where the collective intelligence is shared. Who will need a gatekeeper then?

2

The digital information marketplace and its economics: the end of exclusivity

RICHARD WITHEY

Summary

The digital change does not just concern information. It permeates every aspect of life, from the way we study, learn and educate, to the way we shop, acquire information, gossip, interact, find partners and accumulate wealth. So why not take into account all aspects of communication in deciding which way to go with the services being provided? Business models that have long supported the information industry by creating an audience and methods of delivery are undergoing seismic (some would argue cataclysmic) change, so those who ignore it do so at their peril. Too many years ago, the author, as a fresh-faced library school student, was required to study the workings of the book publishing industry, even to the extent of setting up and printing pages from a hand-press, and learning the meaning of terms such as verso, flyleaf, copyright and perfect binding. The recipients of these black arts were then known as readers, united by a commonality of interest largely unchanged since the days when Wynkyn de Worde, from his press below St Brides, published 25 books in a single year (1509, a year of uncommonly good gossip). The exclusivity created by the ownership of the printing press is over and gone forever. This chapter explains why that matters.

The changing world of publishing

The current threats and opportunities faced by traditional print news and media publishers in the face of digital delivery and content generation systems and applications are becoming well documented, though still subject to some dispute within the publishing industries. Notably, the same debates are taking place in the magazine, broadcasting, book and music publishing markets with equal ferocity. One thing characterizes all of these industries, however, and that is the level of structural change being brought about by the changing nature of the consumer. These industries, having flourished for many decades by understanding very well their own market segments and exploiting their differences, are looking more and more like each other, and the effects of these market breakdowns will prove to be seismic. A student of any of these industries, when asked the fundamental question: 'What is broadcasting?', 'What is consumer publishing?', 'What is music publishing?' or 'What is book publishing?' would find it much more difficult to answer that question in 2008 than they would have in, say 1988. A mere 20 years have begun to alter the landscape of information creation and delivery beyond recognition.

Before the digital revolution, nothing much changed in publishing, and if it did, it changed slowly: publishers were used to ways of doing things that had in effect changed little since the Renaissance, and all publishing disciplines felt comfortable, familiar and somewhat exclusive. The fuss caused by the arrival of Penguin's first paperback in 1935 was understandable – it was practically the only significant change in the book publishing industry for almost the whole of the 20th century. And it is significant that practically all innovations in newspaper production methods after Walter's introduction of steam presses in *The Times* from 1814 onwards were evolutionary rather than disruptive (the Walter Press, a culmination of the steam and rotary press, did not arrive until 1869). Even disruption brought about by the introduction of computer typesetting and direct entry systems in the 1980s was largely confined to production methods rather than to the means of distribution and consumption, bringing scale efficiencies rather than revolution.

Traditionally, in publishing, capital costs have been relatively high and newcomers have found market entry difficult against established players.

This has been largely true of all publishing disciplines, including music, and quite often it has been the means of distribution as well as the means of production that have posed high barriers in terms of both cost and exclusivity. Recently in his Guardian column, Charles Arthur argued persuasively that 'at its heart the internet is a distribution medium', and that distribution will replace content as 'king', for as he sees it: 'content sources are as vast as the web; the distribution sources, limited to telecoms companies' (Arthur, 2008). There is much merit in this argument, for as he also points out, quite a number of the largest companies in the FTSE 100 are telecommunications companies, and although there are a number of media-based, content-producing companies, some of these such as emap are coming out of the FTSE 100 through break-up and shrinking profit margins. Interestingly too, it is those companies that are successfully combining content and programming skills with digitally-led means of distribution that appear to have the strongest positions: for example, companies such as BSkyB, with its quadruple play, time-shifted Sky+ and its See, Speak, Surf offering.

With the arrival of the web the move to digital began to involve consumers, and publishers face changes of significant proportions that may create new paradigms from which all publishers, in all markets and disciplines, can learn. For example, if publishers doubt that things are changing rapidly (and surprisingly, it is apparent that some still do), they have only to look to the music and newspaper industries, where changes to distribution channels and formats have had and are having a direct impact on business models.

Firstly, and most importantly, the way consumers approach and consume information is changing, as many user surveys show. The August 2007 British Market Research Bureau (BMRB) Internet Monitor shows a clear shift in the relative percentages of time spent on different media by consumers – and this has been the case across a number of Internet Monitors recently. They show clearly that (among internet users aged 15+) time spent online is second only to television (BMRB, 2007).

The changes brought about by digital adoption among consumers and the use of social networking are truly structural and systemic, whatever some industry apologists say about 'cyclical downturns'. Chapter 5, on 'The psychology of the digital information consumer', outlines in considerable detail the phenomenal growth in penetration of the internet and the uses to which it is being put, and the evidence shows very clearly that nothing short of a revolution is taking place in household adoption of digital communications technologies. For example, Figure 2.1, from the UK Office of Communications (Ofcom, 2007a), shows not only the significant growth in the proportion of individuals taking up digital communications technologies but also that, as penetration rises, prices (and the proportion of household income spent on them) drop.

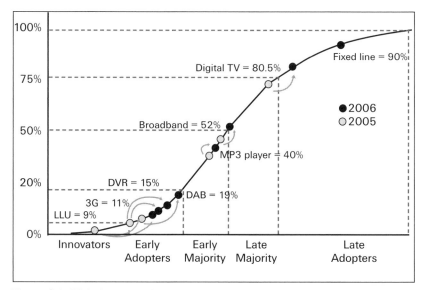

Figure 2.1   Digital communications technologies take-up, 2005 and 2006 proportion of individuals (%)[1] (Source: Ofcom, 2007a)

[1] All figures relate to the end of Q1 2007 except for 3G which is end of 2006. All figures are measured as a proportion of individuals except for 3G, which represents the proportion of mobile subscribers, LLU ('local loop unbundling') which represents the proportion of premises in unbundled areas and DTV, which represents the proportion of homes with a digital television reception device on the main set.

Real monthly household spend on communications services fell for the second year running in 2006, to £92.65, down 1.5% in real terms on 2005, with telecoms spend continuing to account for the lion's share; competitive pressure on fixed and mobile voice played a large part in the reduction. Consumer spend per household on television services also fell slightly year-on-year in real terms (Ofcom, 2007a).

Moreover the time spent using these digital delivery devices is increasing and there is a corresponding drop in the use of some traditional devices such as analogue TV. Also, the data in Table 2.1 reveals a trend away from fixed to mobile devices for digital access, a trend that is now accelerating rapidly with the arrival of devices like the iPhone, the iPod Touch, and wider adoption of 3G platforms by operators. This is clearly illustrated by the Ofcom telecoms industry key metrics in Table 2.1, which show a marked decline in the installation of fixed lines (and a significant decline in market share of fixed revenues held by industry giants such as British Telecom) together with a marked rise in areas such as active mobile and 3G connections and of course in internet connections (Ofcom, 2007b).

Table 2.1 UK telecoms industry key metrics (Source: Ofcom, 2007b)

UK telecoms industry	2002	2003	2004	2005	2006
Total telecoms retail revenue (£bn)	32.3	34.4	36.3	37.9	38.5
Total telecoms wholesale revenue (£bn)	8.6	8.8	8.6	8.3	8.5
Telecoms service revenue (£bn)	40.9	43.1	44.8	46.2	47.0
Average weekly household spend on telecom services (£)	60.7	64.2	66.7	65.7	64.7
Fixed access and calls revenues (£bn)	11.8	11.4	10.7	10.0	9.6
BT share of fixed revenues (%)	71.6	71.1	68.9	66.6	63.0
Proportion of unbundled exchanges (%)	–	–	–	12.4	23.3
Fixed lines (millions)	35.2	35.0	34.6	34.1	33.6
Mobile retail revenues (£bn)	9.0	10.5	12.0	13.0	13.9
Active mobile connections per 100 population	82.6	88.0	99.5	109.1	116.6
Active 3G mobile connections per 100 population	–	0.4	4.3	7.7	13.4
Internet connections per 100 population	18.9	22.2	25.1	26.0	27.6
Broadband connections per 100 population	2.3	5.2	10.2	16.5	21.7

In the individual industries affected by these trends, the traditional business models are beginning to suffer. In the newspaper industry, for example, the picture of business support for publishing has been a simple and, for the participants, a happy one (see Figure 2.2 overleaf).

The audiences, or consumers, were passive participants in this cycle, in that they provided a heterogeneous mass of market opportunities cloaked in editorial output. It was a system with high barriers to entry and costly distribution mechanisms, but for the publishers who were engaged in it, margins were good. Outlets for advertisers have been channelled through intermediaries in press and broadcast and have provided somewhat imponderable Return on Investment (ROI), but the fact is if you wanted to sell or market a service or product you had to reach your potential customer through the accepted mass market channels: print, TV, radio, outdoor marketing, direct marketing or cinema advertising.

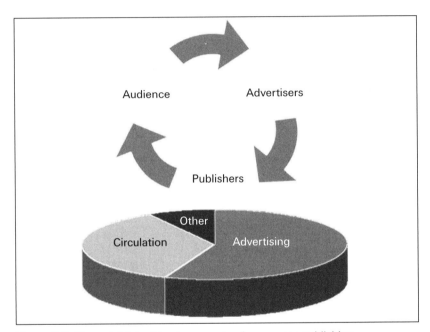

Figure 2.2 The established business cycle of consumer publishing

The very rapid growth in consumer adoption of web access has led to an equally rapid process of these revenue streams becoming eroded by the new digital channels, and the advertisers, after a faltering start largely caused by the confusion of the dot.com bubble and crash of 1999–2001, have been quick to adopt these new channels and will continue to do so, as the latest World Association of Newspapers data shows in Figure 2.3 (WAN, 2007).

Set against this current and anticipated growth is the fact that, overall, traditional advertising spend can be adversely affected. In the UK, for example, Internet Advertising Bureau survey figures for the first half of 2007 show that overall the UK advertising market only grew by 3.1% year-on-year, and, as online advertising grew by 41.3% (a typical growth figure in fact over the last several years), press, TV, radio, cinema and direct mail advertising all declined (IAB, 2007). Most significantly, in terms of structural changes, over half of the UK spend on online advertising went on Search, an area notably dominated by new media organizations and in which traditional publishers have made few inroads.

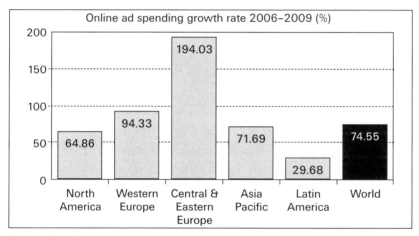

Figure 2.3 Advertisers switch to the web (Source: WAN, 2007)

Most newspaper groups, worldwide, depend on advertising for between one-third and two-thirds of their revenues, and few traditional print publishers in this sector could survive without a healthy flow of advertisers. Yet more and more agency advertising dollars are being diverted, at the request of the clients, towards online channels, where advertisers are beginning to understand they can get more accountability and a better return on investment. As more and more of their potential customers connect through high-speed, always-on broadband (and, as can be seen above, costs of doing so come down), advertisers are beginning to switch their allegiance. Also their ability to put together compelling, high quality advertising messages and to deliver them online is vastly increased by broadband prevalence. Over 90% of UK home internet users now connect through a broadband line and over 50% of UK adults have such access at home. Witness the rapid adoption, following its re-launch at the start of 2008 (to work within web browsers), of the BBC iPlayer (which requires a high-speed link) and *Screen Digest*'s anticipated number of 2.8 billion streams and downloads by 2012 (Kiss, 2008).

Examples from other content industries

Despite these trends, publishers in every sector have been slow to respond to changing market conditions which are being brought about by digital access. Traditional publishers in other sectors such as STM and trade book publishing may witness these events with a shrug and a sense of thankfulness that they are not exposed to the raw power of the consumer and the advertising market. To some extent, this has been because the supporting infrastructure of content creation and distribution has been, as described above, comfortable and well understood, and also because it has attractive margins. Traditional publishers have also been slow to respond to the very rapid breaking down of high-cost entry barriers in their respective publishing and distribution industries. And yet before them stands the all too vivid example of the music industry.

Who could have predicted that, in the few years the iPod has existed, it has given Apple a share equal to almost 90% of the US market for legal music downloads? Traditional music distributors have first blustered, then sued, then acquired in the face of new social and peer-to-peer threats to high-cost music distribution such as Napster. However the real lesson for all publishers lies in the way Apple set about winning this share of the market, by closely synthesizing the technology of its admittedly 'cool' device with the iTunes Store and its content. For the consumer, who is now central to the process rather than peripheral to it, they are synonymous, they work seamlessly, they are cost-effective and the consumer is in full control.

No one in the retail book trade should be surprised by the success of the iPod. It is quite clear from the early history of web development in the 1990s that the first internet trading of non-virtual commodities centred on books, and though Amazon did not turn its first full-year profit until 2003, it has become a giant of commodity search and delivery on the web. Moreover the methods of search combined with user recommendation and virtual bookshelves that stocked themselves based on user behaviour were pioneered by Amazon, have been widely copied and improved on by other web media pioneers (most notably Google) and have led pretty directly (certainly conceptually) to blogs and wikis.

Audible.com followed Amazon pretty smartly by pioneering the downloading of audible texts, and became the precursor to the iPod. It could be argued that these early developments in book distribution through the web, in which 'early adopters' participated in online purchasing of non-virtual items for the first time, led the way for technology to change consumer behaviour fundamentally.

In tandem the revolution in music distribution kick-started by Napster has been almost wholly consumer-led: the line from peer-to-peer linked geeks swapping favourite tracks, through to the ready availability (and relative cheapness) of broadband access, to the use of these networks for film and video distribution, is a fast, straight, undeviating track. Meanwhile the publishing industries have, largely, not participated until forced to, and when they do, too often the effects are muted. Moreover the weaknesses in the response of traditional publishers to the rise of the web since 1993 are now beginning to show in their market positions. As this chapter is being written, EMI music announced job cuts of at least 1500 to save costs of up to £200 million a year, against a background of a slump in its share of album sales in the previous year from 15% to 9% (Andrews, 2008). Emap appears to have a buyer for its radio and magazine businesses (having earlier agreed to put the whole business up for sale following a generally lacklustre market perform-ance) and will now focus on its B2B (business-to-business) operations in Emap Communications (Allen, 2007). Generally, media owners complain regularly about the perceived mark-down of their stocks by analysts.

So already, in one short decade of growth, we have before us two stark examples of seismic change in business economics facing two significant publishing industries: music publishing and distribution, and consumer publishing in the shape of newspapers and magazines. Those in other publishing industries who feel they are less exposed to, and therefore largely immune from, changes in economic forces driven by consumers cannot afford any sense of complacency. Just because a business is not directly dependent on, say, advertising support it does not follow that similar change is not already knocking on the door marked profitability. Consumers of all kinds are essentially learning, and gaining from, new forms of behaviour in their purchase of information commodities, and their expectations are being driven by digital formats and digital means of delivery.

Newspaper publishing

To return to newspaper publishing as an example of perceived threats (and opportunities) to an industry, some 22 key figures were recently asked by the World Association of Newspapers to identify many of the recognized threats and attributes of digital change and their perceived impact on their industry's future success. These included the following observations:

- Availability is increasingly important – people do not always buy what they like, but instead what is at hand. 24/7 is becoming the norm.
- Infinite choice – too many options makes it hard to decide what product/service to buy.
- Consumer power – the customer is taking control over brands and media flows on the internet (blogs, etc.).
- Consumer-generated ads – customers creating, and distributing, commercial messages.
- Social networks – Facebook and other social networks are of growing importance.
- Audience fragmentation – more channels and more content providers mean a thinning out of audiences.
- User-generated content – more people create and share their content with others (e.g. blogs). User-generated content provides opportunities for self-expression and social interaction.
- New demands on sales – selling advertisements is becoming increasingly important, and difficult, as there are so many media channels.

- Digital media offers better measures – digital media have an increasingly important advantage of being able to measure the impact of advertisements, clicks, transactions, etc.
- Newspapers are becoming exclusive – newspapers with high quality measures can become more expensive and thus address only an exclusive class.

Quoted from World Association of Newspapers press release
(WAN, 2008)

There were many positive attributes also recognized by the group, but these all depend largely on the ability of the industry to reinvent itself, and to respond to the challenge of the new, entirely digital forms of publishing and media.

Many of these attributes, good and bad, also apply to other forms of publishing, and are equally disruptive. Most publishers, it can be assumed, are ignorant of the issues raised by Christensen et al. (2007) in their theories of disruptive technology, which are explored below. They need, however, to be made aware of these issues, because publishing industries as a whole are undergoing almost a classic example of this in action. Blind-sided by the very real attributes of their current technologies and distribution platforms to deliver healthy margins and aided by a high level of consolidation in publishing that has to some extent papered over deep cracks in its very foundations, they have been able until recently to ignore the potent disruptive threats of new distribution channels created by new technologies.

Change or die?

How have publishers reacted to these threats? Consumer media were certainly the first to face up to the challenge of the internet. In fact publishers of newspapers and magazines responded quickly to the advent of web publishing following the release of the Mosaic web browser in 1993. Though, in retrospect, their collective reaction could fairly be described as mixed at best, they were among the early adopters and many of the first websites were news based. Unfortunately they were driven by some of the early projections of growth drawn up by analysts and consultancies on which they heavily depend for guidance. While these early- to mid-1990s projections were largely accurate in their forecasts of the number of people who would be likely to adopt the web as a major communications tool, they missed two very important guide posts. No-one made it clear how very different margins would appear in digital publishing compared to print publishing, and almost everyone missed, or underestimated, the social revolution in publishing that largely came about after 2000.

The lessons now being learned by newspaper and magazine publishers in the consumer sphere are that massive changes in distribution are brought about by digital (and particularly wireless) distribution, and these have a profound effect on the business model. Everyone, including consumer publishers, spent the first years of the web worrying about the technological impact, and were largely happy to leave developments to their more technically oriented staff, who focused on how to digitize content produced by large print factories. However, as we can now see, clearly the biggest impact of digital change is on the nature and shape of the audience, on the distribution, and access, to the audience and on the changed requirements that audiences now have. Consequently business models, almost overnight, have become transactional, incremental and temporary in nature, a fact which new media organizations such as Yahoo! and Google understood implicitly from day one.

This is not to argue that the publishing industry has been asleep during these developments. Trade publishers, for example, have now woken up to new opportunities for audience reach and marketing, such as the HarperCollins Browse Inside (similar to Amazon's A9.com technology, which allows users to search inside books). Many are experimenting with content delivered to the Irex Iliad (which at the time of writing contains over 49,000 books in the MobiPocket format), the Sony eBook, which is taking a very similar line to that of the iPod, with an eBook store for downloads, or the recently introduced Amazon Kindle, which already boasts over 80,000 available books, journals, newspapers and blogs. Criticism levelled at these kinds of devices usually centres on their cost, size and incompatibility with similar devices. Most early adopters like the organic light-emitting diode

(OLED) technology that without backlight allows material to be read in any light just like print matter. However the real point of difference between them will emerge as the distribution methods for the content. Whatever changes in format come about as a result of market feedback, one can confidently predict from other distributive lessons taught by the web that only those devices that can seamlessly and wirelessly deliver new content will survive. If any device is to have ubiquitous market appeal on a global basis, it will have to deliver content anywhere, anyhow and effortlessly (on the part of the consumer). The early experiments with Printing on Demand (POD) for books, such as the Espresso machine first used in a retail setting by the World Bank's InfoShop, may not have been universally acclaimed, but the views of an experienced publisher such as Jason Epstein, former Editorial Director of Random House, may be perceptive: 'By the time all books are digitized over the next few years, we will have replaced the 500-year-old Gutenberg system. Everyone will have access to the machine and will be able to download any book ever printed' (http://web.worldbank.org).

It does appear however that the core questions about the sustainability of existing publishing businesses raised by Christensen et al. (2007) are not being addressed. With the idea of 'disruptive technology', Christensen argues that good companies can and do fail, and that this happens not in spite of their core competence but because of it. It can be seen, in fact, from some reliable market evidence over the last ten years that what could be deemed good business practice, such as focusing investment on the most profitable products that are currently in demand by the best customers, will, when faced with disruptive innovation, ultimately damage the business. As a result, in newspaper groups in developed internet economies (not yet in developing markets), margins are suffering, circulation of paid-for titles is declining and editors are coming to terms with the fact that there are other kinds of consumers out there with different expectations about how they want to consume and pay for information. For example, recent results of the British Social Attitudes Survey, published annually and reported in *The Guardian* show that only 20% of graduates regularly read a quality newspaper, compared with 50% in 1986, and that the decline of print readership has not been taken up by the internet. Among those who do not read a paper regularly, only 3% regularly consult a newspaper website.

The possibility that newspapers will disappear because of increased use of digital media as an alternative is posited by some, most notably Philip Meyer (2004, cited in Jenkins, 2005), who has predicted the date the last one will be read: 'An academic observer, Philip Meyer, has calculated that at the present rate of fall the last newspaper will be read in April, 2040 (and still looking as if it was designed in the 1930s)'.

In fact newspaper readership has actually been in decline in the UK since the 1950s although there are still over 17 million newspaper readers each day – albeit 2 million of those are now free ones.

Much more worrying for publishers though are the levels of valuations being applied to media companies in developed economies. The sale of the once-powerful Knight-Ridder titles to McClatchy and the subsequent downgrading of the group titles is the most vivid example of this, but also instructive is what is happening to the Tribune Group and its figurehead title, the *Los Angeles Times*. Recently bought by Sam Zell, the new proprietor has signalled his intention to privatize the Tribune Group on the grounds that 'Most investors think the newspaper industry is going to be run over by the Internet' and that meeting the needs of analysts and shareholders is inappropriate in an industry that has to reinvent itself and needs to think for the long term (Carpenter, 2007).

The fact most newspaper managements are exercised about is that analysts underestimate their inherent valuations, and in most industries this would be seen as an indicator of a mature market in irreversible decline. Tapscott (2000), like Zell, also believes this – the theory that the structural capital of newspaper groups is often at odds with current and developing market requirements – and suggests that 'human capital', 'structural capital', and 'customer capital' should be recast as 'digital capital' (Tapscott et al., 2000). The question remains whether publishers of all kinds will agree with what Tapscott suggests, and identify and accumulate digital capital. Can they, for example in the newspaper industry, counteract both the trend towards an increasingly ageing reader demographic for traditional print newspapers, and a failure by younger demographics to take up newspaper readership in any great numbers – the group characterized by the Berkman Centre for

Internet and Society at Harvard Law School as 'digital natives' (www. digitalnative.org)?

Some consumer publishers have begun again to respond, after the 'phoney war' of the dot.com boom and crash. The News Corporation investment in MySpace networks looks as though it may have transformed the company, focusing as it does on audience rather than technology. This is perceptive: in a Deloitte and Touche Survey of 30 digital decision-makers in consumer publishing houses, technology came a very poor fourth in a ranking of the top five drivers for digital success, behind marketing and business model imperatives. The main driver for success, by some margin, was perceived to be meeting changing customer needs (Deloitte and AOP, 2006).

The difficulty for most traditional publishers arises from identifying these needs in an increasingly fragmented market. In the early 1990s most publishers' discussions around the threat of digital incursion into their businesses usually involved three concepts:

1   Fragmentation of audience, as new channels to market emerged.
2   Disintermediation, as increasingly advertisers, and indeed product and service providers, could reach markets via the web directly.
3   Personalization, where discrete niche audiences could gather together with a set of commonalities that made them attractive to advertisers.

For publishing and broadcasting industries which had grown up around the concept of combining mass audiences together under broad banners – 'Times reader', 'Channel 4 watcher', 'Coronation Street fan', and so on – these concepts could be dynamite. For a while it looked as though the concepts described by Charles Handy in his perceptive view of the future *The Empty Raincoat* had arrived in a rush, particularly his vision of the organization, which had been like a castle, becoming more like a condominium: 'an association of temporary residents gathered together for their mutual convenience', and 'a collection of permanent and temporary project groups existing more in a computer than in a set of shared offices' (Handy, 1994). His vision, while principally applied to the workplace, was an effective prediction of the way social networks operate.

However in the mid-1990s the social network, on any significant scale, was still some way off, and it seemed for a while that the dot.com crash had put paid to any forebodings by publishers. These forebodings have re-emerged significantly with the appearance of content-sharing websites such as Flickr and YouTube and the emergence of large-scale social networks like Facebook, MySpace and Bebo. Significantly a recent report by The Book-sellers Association, on the digital challenges and opportunities faced by book publishers, places the consumer at the centre of things, rather than at the end of the supply chain as in the past, but also notes that 'the distributors' business models are still not well-developed for the consumer market' and that the 'product-centric' and 'mass-market' supply chain becomes 'customer-centric' and 'direct-market' focused in the digital world (Daniels, 2006, 33).

It could be argued that a number of technology developments in media and publishing have come up against Christensen et al.'s (2007) theories of disruptive innovation, and that the ground for these changes was laid some time before the advent of the consumer web, led by a number of fundamental changes in telecommunications and computing, including:

1   The migration from mainframe computing to client–server computing and the eventual advent of micro-computing in the consumer marketplace.
2   The arrival from the 1970s onwards of widely available 'shareware' delivered via dial-up services to the desktop.
3   The migration from fixed-line telephony to mobile telephony, and the concurrent migration from voice to data.
4   The concentration since the mid-1980s on 'value-added' communications services, again through the arrival of new players to replace the old 'pots-and-pans' telephony providers, resulting in the creation of the 'baby-bells' in the US, and the near melt-down of British Telecom before it began to respond.
5   Finally, aided by the advent of the internet itself, the arrival of open system platforms and collaborative software development, which really took off when the graphical web brought an avalanche of consumer applications.

PC penetration in developed economy households had shown some signs of reaching a plateau before significant web access (and particularly broadband) arrived. Typically this plateau was around 50% of (generally more affluent) households. However the World Association of Newspapers predicts (using a composite of analysts' data from a number of sources) global broadband household penetration of 433 million by 2010 (from 30 million in 2001), with 75% of households having at least one PC. And, despite the early dominance of the US in the take-up of these technologies, both Europe and Asia have already surpassed the US in numbers of internet users. Only 28% of the global population of internet users of over 1 billion people is aged above 40 (WAN, 2007).

The applicability of these developments to social networks is clear. Ubiquitous broadband access is here, increasingly over broadband mobile networks, with falling prices (in real terms) for access, connectivity, technology and services. Broadband allows not only fast access, and always-on technology, but also the sharing and production of content at the widest possible level. Many of the most successful web companies have arisen as a result of social groups (often young demographics too) wanting a solution for the sharing of content. YouTube is the clearest example of this and of its applicability to new forms of niche-driven mass markets.

Why does this matter to publishers – of all traditions?

As Rupert Murdoch said, in his 2005 speech to the American Society of Editors:

> We need to realize that the next generation of people accessing news and information, whether from newspapers or any other source, have a different set of expectations about the kind of news they will get, including when and how they will get it, where they will get it from, and who they will get it from . . . My two young daughters . . . will be digital natives. They'll never know a world without ubiquitous broadband internet access.
>
> (News Corporation, 2005)

Why are the digital natives different? Firstly, and very importantly from a structural viewpoint, this is the first technology roll-out that is consumer-led rather than business-led, and the consumer is beginning to control the publishing agenda. Secondly, all readers and information users, in every publishing sector, are fundamentally consumers, and learn their habits in the wider marketplace – a whole new level of expectation is being established through instant access, downloadability, the ability to time-shift consumption and involvement in the creative process.

Particularly in relation to web access, mobile access and social network usage, consumers are learning new patterns of behaviour in information access, and at a young age, then adopting these throughout life, and it is clear also that older generations, once they adopt digital media, learn and exercise the same habits and patterns of behaviour.

It is also clear that consumer take-up of broadband drives wholly new business models with significantly different margins. The phenomenon of such rapid change brought about, effectively, by what some would describe as the 'wisdom of the crowd', places intolerable burdens on levels of shareholder expectation and delivery.

There are many questions still to be answered about the shape and direction of our future publishing industries. Some of the answers that emerge may not be welcome:

> Newspaper executives and analysts say that it could take five to 10 years for the industry's finances to stabilize and that many of the papers that survive will be smaller and will practice less ambitious journalism.
>
> Some companies may look for buyers, but it is not clear how much of a market for newspapers remains. The first test will come from the Sun-Times Media Group, which announced Monday that after suffering deep losses and closing several small weekly papers, it would try to sell any assets it could, including its flagship paper, *The Sun-Times*.
>
> (Pérez-Peña, 2008)

Whatever solutions to industry restructuring problems do emerge, they will have to operate in a new and very different landscape, where consumers, not publishers, appear to dictate the market. Those who have read Malcolm Gladwell's *Tipping Point: how little things can make a big difference* (Little Brown, 2000) may feel it was prescient in terms of what has happened since then with the incredible growth of social networks, blogging and other forms of socially interactive publishing; the fact that you could, if you had an Amazon Kindle, buy and be reading Gladwell's book within one minute may be another tipping point.

Others may prefer the recent viewpoint of Scott Karp, who claims:

> You can explain the power of social networks and the 'social graphs' in terms of links – every Facebook profile has links to other Facebook profiles. Same with MySpace. And LinkedIn – get it?
>
> Journalists and PR professionals, the influence brokers of traditional media, have lost a huge degree of influence on the web in large part because they don't link to anything. While traditional media brands are still powerful channels on the web, they are losing influence every day to the link-driven web network – journalists and PR professionals can no longer depend on controlling these former monopoly channels to exert influence online. . . . Influence on the web is all about connectivity – the larger the network, the more powerful the links.
>
> (Karp, 2008)

Perhaps the last word should go to one of the most influential bloggers (or connectors) on the web today, Jeff Jarvis, who blogs frequently on this subject in his BuzzMachine:

> Let people – no, encourage – people to distribute your stuff for you. You can no longer spend a huge marketing budget to get people to come to you . . . If you're not being remixed, you're not part of the conversation. And the conversation is the platform of today.
>
> (Jarvis, 2006)

References

Allen, K. (2007) Emap sells magazines and radio businesses to Bauer for £1.14bn, *The Guardian*, 7 December,
www.guardian.co.uk/business/2007/dec/07/emapbusiness.emap.

Andrews, A. (2008) Guy Hands's cost cuts could save £200m at EMI, *The Times*, 15 January,
http://business.timesonline.co.uk/tol/business/industry_sectors/media/article31 87632.ece#cid=OTC-RSS&attr=1185799.

Arthur, C. (2008) The online money is in distribution, not content, *The Guardian*, 10 January, www.guardian.co.uk/technology/2008/jan/10/3.

BMRB (British Market Research Bureau) (2007) *Internet Monitor* (August).

Carpenter, D. (2007) Billionaire Zell: newspapers have been complacent, *USA Today*, 25 October.

Christensen, C. M., Baumann, H., Ruggles, R. and Sadtler, T. (2007) Disruptive Innovation for Social Change, *Harvard Business Review*, **84** (12), 94–101.

Daniels, M. (2006) *Brave New World, Digitisation of Content: the opportunities for booksellers and The Booksellers Association, Report to the BA Council from the DOC Working Group*, The Booksellers Association of the United Kingdom and Ireland Ltd,
www.booksellers.org.uk/documents/digitisation_of_content/Brave%20New%20World.pdf.

Deloitte and AOP (2006) *Turn the Page: the net benefit of digital publishing*, Deloitte and Touche LLP,
www.deloitte.com/dtt/cda/doc/content/UK_TMT_Turn%20the%20page.pdf.

Handy, C. (1994) *The Empty Raincoat*, Hutchinson Business.

IAB (2007) *Online Adspend Study H1 1007*, Internet Advertising Bureau.

Jarvis, J. (2006) WWGD: the news API, *BuzzMachine*, (18 October),
www.buzzmachine.com/2006/10/18/wwgd-the-news-api/.

Jenkins, S. (2005) Under my keyboard the desk shakes. The bloggers are on the march, *The Times*, 11 March,
www.timesonline.co.uk/tol/comment/columnists/simon_jenkins/article424565.ece.

Karp, S. (2008) *Influentials on the Web are People with the Power to Link*, Publishing 2.0, (28 January), http://publishing2.com/2008/01/28/influentials-on-the-web-are-people-with-the-power-to-link/.

Kiss, J. (2008) iPlayer driving online TV, report says, *The Guardian*, 6 February, www.guardian.co.uk/media/2008/feb/06/bbc.digitalmedia.

Little Brown (2000) www.nytimes.com/2008/02/07/business/media/07paper.html.

Meyer, P. (2004) *The Vanishing Newspaper*, University of Missouri Press.

News Corporation (2005) Speech by Rupert Murdoch to the American Society of Newspaper Editors, 13 April, www.newscorp.com/news/news_247.html.

Ofcom (2007a) *The Communications Market 2007; 1 Converging Communications Market*, Office of Communications, 16.

Ofcom (2007b) *The Communications Market 2007: 4 Telecommunications*, Office of Communications, 255.

Pérez-Peña, R. (2008) An industry imperiled by falling profits and shrinking ads, *The New York Times*, 7 February.

Tapscott, D., Lowy, A. and Ticoll, D. (2000) *Digital Capital: harnessing the power of business webs*, Harvard Business School Press.

WAN (2007) *World Digital Media Trends 2007*, World Association of Newspapers.

WAN (2008) *Envisioning the Future of the Newspaper*, World Association of Newspapers.

Ward, L. and Carvel, J. (2008) Goodbye married couples, hello alternative family arrangements, *The Guardian*, 23 January, www.guardian.co.uk/society/2008/jan/23/socialtrends.

3

The e-shopper: the growth of the informed purchaser

CHRIS RUSSELL

Summary

When the internet started to make its influence felt on the commercial world there was an adage that was quickly adopted as being 'true': an internet year for commercial planning purposes was seven weeks long. Therefore a traditional five-year plan would last no longer than 35 weeks. Decisions on capital investment, organizational structure, and marketing and sales plans would all have to be taken at the same pace. To miss the opportunity would have far-reaching consequences on an organization's future – possibly its existence. This is as true for e-information providers as it is for e-retailers. That speed of change provided by the internet has had a profound influence on traditional retailers. They have been stung into action by the success (and threat) of new organizations such as Amazon.com, a major information provider after all, and their influence on the 'bricks and mortar' shopper. Changes in consumer shopping behaviour have been swift and decisive and have altered the face of retailing (including associated information services) forever. The doom-mongers of the dot.com crash have been proved wrong. The internet is here to stay and it has changed the boundaries within which a business or organization has to operate. It would be a brave person (or fool) who believes the same will not happen in the information marketplace.

This chapter looks at the history of the development of the e-shopper – mostly in the UK – and the development of the shopper journey – their likes, dislikes, and expected standards, in order that we can better understand the information consumer. In addition, it looks at the influence that the e-shopper has had on other elements of organizations and demands made on their organizational skills. It shows that the e-shopper is driving changes in markets that traditionally ran at the pace of the old five-year plans – and concludes that the e-shopper, who after all conducts a good deal of product research, will demand the same changes in other areas of internet usage, like that for scholarly information. Having an understanding of the pace of change will help information professionals understand the need for their organizational planning to increase in scope and rapidity and to embrace technological and behavioural evolution – or ignore it at their peril.

Background

Electronic commerce, commonly known as e-commerce or eCommerce, consists of the buying and selling of products or services over electronic systems such as the internet and other computer networks (Wikipedia, 2008). This relatively new concept has been embraced by a new kind of computer user – not academics, scholars or scientists, but people who are using the internet for personal use, gain, communication, research and, increasingly, shopping. Therefore a study of e-shoppers provides the information professional and publisher with a broader understanding of their digital users and, importantly, the 'new' users who now constitute a large part of their audience. E-shoppers have no unusual demographic (other than they have to be old enough to have a credit or bank card) or particular financial boundaries, and are collectively leading a revolution in consumer behaviour that is having a profound effect on organizations and their future. This behavioural change has been driven by a combination of technological advances and physical and emotional changes in lifestyles.

This chapter will mainly concentrate on experience gained from the UK but will also refer to other countries and experiences, notably the United States.

History of e-commerce[1]

In 1990 when Tim Berners-Lee invented 'hyperlinked' documents residing on networked computers – the basis of today's world wide web – little could he have realized the paradigm shift in consumer behaviour that his invention was to cause in the years to follow. It was not, however, until some four years later, in 1994, when Marc Andreessen, Jamie Zawinski and others developed the 'click and point' browser – Netscape – and set the precedent for 'free' software, that the environment for e-commerce was established and set to blossom. Thus in 1995 eBay conducted its first auction and Jeff Bezo opened Amazon in his spare room – and the dot.com 'boom' commenced with fledgling organizations operating with 'land grab' mentality both for consumers and investment cash. The important concept of 'disintermediation' (loosely defined and understood as 'cutting out the middleman') and lower transaction costs suddenly became industry watchwords for the future. Further technological breakthroughs have taken place that have fuelled expansion – in 1996 Microsoft launched 'Merchant Server' combining shopping cart, product database and secure back-end payment modules. The e-retail infrastructure was in place and growth-over-profit business models became commonplace.

In spite of the financial readjustment of the dot.com crash of March 2000 and some high-profile financial failures in the UK such as Boo.com and, in the USA, Webvan and Pets.com, an undercurrent of increasing internet use and online purchasing continued. Consumers harboured an impression of cheaper prices and so continued to persevere with internet use. Confidence improved and consumers learned to enjoy an improving site usage experience resulting in increased use of the medium for product research and, in turn, sales. In 2002, online sales reached 4% of the total UK retail pot while £1 billion was spent online for the first time in one month alone (November). By 2004 this had grown to 6.8% of all retail sales and £1.6 billion was spent in December alone. By 2005 UK users were online for longer than they watched TV and 8.8% of all retail sales were conducted online with £2.3 billion being spent in December.

Continually encouraged by retailers who now competed for consumers through promotion and improved site usability, 15% of all retail sales were conducted online in 2007 (total UK retail sales was estimated at £300 billion). Online retail sales for the year were estimated at £46.6 billion, an increase of 54% on the £30.2 billion spent in the previous year. During December alone £5.4 billion was spent – itself an increase of 50% on the previous year. It was estimated that 23 million Britons bought Christmas presents online (eDigitalResearch, Nov–Dec 2007). In the UK the Interactive Media in Retail Group (IMRG)[2] produces an e-retail sales index gleaned from its members (most of the major UK e-retailers). This index charted a 5,213% increase in UK online shopping sales during the 94 months between April 2000 and December 2007 (Figure 3.1), with significant 'spikes' during Christmas sales periods. Interestingly, while online information use has probably mirrored this level of growth, Christmas is the time when use drops off considerably, probably displaced by online shopping activities!

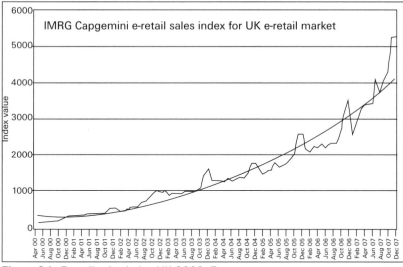

Figure 3.1 E-retail sales index UK 2000–7
(Source: IMRG)

The number of e-shoppers increased nearly seven-fold between 2000 and 2007 (671%) whereas internet users increased by 187% reflecting the increasing trend towards consumers not only using the internet but also purchasing online (see Figure 3.2).

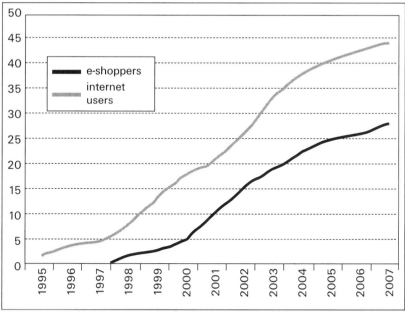

Figure 3.2 The growth of e-shoppers and internet users in the UK (millions)
(Source: IMRG)

During this period US online retail sales remained at less than 5% of overall sales but nonetheless were predicted to grow from $172 billion in 2005 to $329 billion in 2010 with a solid 14% compound annual growth (Johnson, 2005).

The profile of the e-shopper

Research conducted for the Office for National Statistics found that looking for information and using e-mail were the two most common online activities of internet users in 2006 (National Statistics, 2007b). These activities were undertaken by 85% and 81% of adult users respectively in the three months before interview in 2006. Approximately two in five (44%) of the adult population said they had purchased something online for private or personal reasons other than work. The most common items bought by online shoppers in the 12 months before interview were travel and holidays (51%), followed by films, videos and DVDs (42%). Demonstrating greater consumer engagement, nearly one in five (18%) of internet users had sold goods or services over the internet: this was more than double the proportion (7%) in 2003–4.

The majority (70%) of those who had shopped online had not encountered any problems doing so. For those who had, the most common problem was that delivery took longer than expected; this was experienced by 14% of online shoppers (National Statistics, 2007b). Given the popularity of scholarly information e-resources demonstrated in Chapter 6, it would appear that virtual scholars do not experience many problems either.

From an initial male 'early adopter' bias, shoppers visiting e-commerce sites have increasingly moved towards the current UK population gender split of 49% males:51% females with a 56% male:44% female split in 2007 (Table 3.1). Further analysis shows that different types of sites have different gender profiles. For example women prefer to search for their electrical equipment at department stores and high-street chains, whereas men prefer more specialist shops. Analysing a selection of the top electrical retailers, ebuyer, Maplin and Dabs (specialist retailers) are all more popular with men than women, while the opposite is true for more mainstream retailers such as Currys, Carphone Warehouse and Asda Electricals (IMRG, 2008).

The age profile of e-shoppers is, of course, influenced by the availability of payment methods – younger internet users do not have appropriate debit or credit cards – although the recent growth in payment methods such as PayPal and pre-paid debit cards has seen this younger segment of the market

Table 3.1 The gender and age profile of e-shoppers (Source: eDigitalResearch)

Year	2006	2007
Gender		
Male	57%	56%
Female	43%	44%
Age		
Under 18	0.91%	2.47%
18–24	8.37%	9.36%
25–34	20.58%	20.17%
35–44	26.26%	25.49%
45–54	22.21%	21.24%
55–64	15.01%	14.51%
65+	6.66%	6.75%

grow in importance in online shopping terms. This makes the age profile of the e-shopper somewhat older than that of the virtual scholar, where younger users (students) are the majority, but not the heaviest, users.

Navigating the virtual shopping space

E-shoppers, like information shoppers, cross-check. Research conducted in December 2007(eDigitalResearch, Dec 2007–Jan 2008) showed that 88% of e-shoppers will visit more than one site to check a price before purchase. Of these, 88% will visit more than three sites to compare and 21% will visit more than five sites. Some 58% reported using a price comparison site at some stage during the last three months. However, 81% reported using five or less sites to buy their Christmas presents – suggesting that they will visit many sites but buy from a few loyal and trusted ones.

Since 1999, eDigitalResearch has monitored shopper experiences through e-commerce websites. We have identified several key points of the e-shopper journey and have researched each aspect – noting drivers of satisfaction and dissatisfaction – to provide insights into what makes a satisfactory e-shopper journey. This is something that needs to be undertaken for the journey of the digital information consumer.

The e-shopper makes a number of decisions as they journey (or not) through a website (Figure 3.3 overleaf). The journey starts with the initial Home Page – or landing page – moves on to searching and browsing for products, then to the purchase decision, the physical checkout, the receipt and delivery of products and interaction with an organization's customer service.

Searching

Starting with the Home or landing page, search engines play an increasingly important role in finding a site or product and information, particularly as technology has improved with the 'Google-ization' of search functionality. In 2007 approximately a third of internet users used a search engine to find a site – even if they had visited the site before (see Figure 3.4, page 43). In

| Home page | Search Browse Departments | Find Product information? | Shopping basket | Checkout | Delivery and after sales Customer service |

Figure 3.3 The e-shopper journey

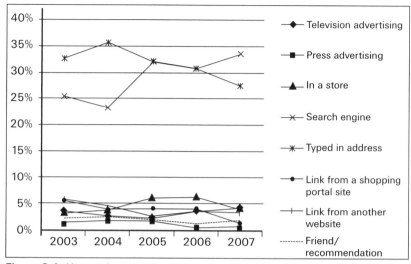

Figure 3.4 How e-shoppers found a major UK electrical online retailer 2003–7
(Source: eDigitalResearch)

2003 this was just a quarter. The search words used to find sites have changed as well. An example is the term 'sale'. According to Hitwise the number of UK consumers searching for post-Christmas sales online more than trebled during the 2007 holiday period. There were 249% more UK internet searches for the term 'sales' for the week ending 29 December 2007 than for the comparable week in 2006. There was also a 200% increase in searches for the term 'sale' over the same period (IMRG, 2008). This is further evidence of volatility and change in the behaviour of the digital consumer mirroring that found in the virtual scholar.

Having found a site – the shop window – successful sites clearly signpost the visitor towards what they want using increasingly 'standard' navigation tools. Very much modelled on Amazon.com, this has become a shop window with a central promotional area, a top navigation bar with clear product or service tabs and a left-hand listing of key and more detailed navigation or product areas (Figure 3.5, overleaf). This is interesting because the navigational system is one originally designed for selling books. E-shoppers look for promotional offers as their expectations are that prices on the internet must be cheaper. Most importantly, however, they look for trust and security as a key reason for continuing to visit a site.

Figure 3.5 Amazon homepage in 2001 (top) and 2008 (bottom) – consistent navigation and key journey signposting that has become an internet 'standard'

Until 2005 it was common for sites to exhibit advanced technological facilities that had the effect of slowing down page loading, which in turn affected a visitor's propensity to continue with the site. There are lessons here for information providers. Consumers want quick wins.

Having established that the site should have what they are looking for, visitors will attempt to find it. Of all the sections contained within a site, search is the most difficult to get right but it is a key factor in user satisfaction. Significantly, it is the area that has taken the longest to catch up with shopper expectations – and even now in 2008 this has *not* been achieved in most cases. Keyword searches are now expected to return results with 'Googlesque' accuracy and users are disappointed with anything less. They do, of course, expect the accuracy they have got used to when they search for information generally. Common mis-spellings and heuristic algorithm based systems are still not commonplace but are expected by users (although they do not know them as such). The latest statistics on how many words people use on search engines show that, on average, they use 2.2 terms per query. In 1994 only 1.3 words were used, so some improvement here; early search facilities mostly failed to impress, were slow and often produced null results – especially (unfortunately) when users knew that a product was featured on a site. Even as early as 2001, users expected multi-word search facilities – keyword searches often failed since databases were full of jargon-based words with users not understanding (and therefore not using) the heading, e.g. toilet tissue (used by the site) v. toilet rolls or paper (used by the shopper).

During 2002 it was clear that those sites that offered a range of search methods were preferred so that users could find and select the fastest method to suit them. Speed is often preferred to accuracy. As late as 2003, the 'pure play' sites (selling online only), such as Amazon, eBay, and figleaves, continued to outperform 'bricks' sites and introduced more sophisticated search engines. During late 2004 some traditional retailer sites, e.g. major catalogue sites, like Kays, introduced new product-linked search engines that were more in line with user expectations.

It has always been, and continues to be, the case that user coverage expectations also affect perception of search results, with users expecting to see the full high-street range available online – not always the case even with some key UK e-commerce sites, e.g. Homebase. This leads to shopper confusion (did they put in the wrong terms?) and dissatisfaction. They want to see it all and the web is thought to be an environment in which this is easily accomplished.

Sites still have issues with finding things, except in a number of cases where sites have worked hard at search back-end systems. At the time of writing there are still too many examples of hits being returned that are irrelevant and incorrect. For instance, entering 'American fridge' into the search engine of one major UK retail site will see 'jeans' and 'Jamie Oliver Platters' returned. (The site does sell American fridges.) In addition, products need to be able to be browsed under headings or departments understood by users and not under the jargon-based name given to it by an organization. The outcome of such retrieval problems is that e-shoppers either rate the range offered by the site as 'poor' or blame the search functionality and go elsewhere (only a 'click' away, not a car journey).

Travel example

What follows is an example of the shopping search for those making a travel transaction. It looks at the search function more broadly and covers the frequency of visiting and searching. The internet is rapidly becoming the number one resource for the travel consumer. A study by Google (ComScore, 2007) revealed that 20 million people in the UK utilized search engines for travel information in the first quarter of 2007. The key findings include the following points:

On average, consumers take nearly a month to go from their first search to a purchase. On average, customers make 12 travel-related searches, visit 22 websites and take 29 days from the first time they search until they make a purchase. Almost half of transactions (45%) occur four weeks or more after the first search. The time spent online is lengthy, representing a prolonged opportunity for advertisers to reach and influence consumers while they search for information. This suggests that the digital consumer takes their time, should they wish to, to realize the benefits of considered research.

On average, travellers visit the purchase website 2.5 times. Most shoppers visit the site they eventually purchase from more than once, averaging 2.5 visits. For tour operators this was significantly higher at 3.9%. Just 10% of the transactions take place on the first search referral to a given site, and 38% of transactions happen at four weeks or more after the first visit. Travel companies face a growing challenge to retain the online consumer as the proliferation of competition encourages travel customers to shop around. This alludes to a finding about information promiscuity found in the case of the digital information consumer and discussed in Chapter 6.

Generic search terms play a significant role in the consumer journey to purchase. Of online travel buyers, 54% started the shopping process with a generic product or destination search term, and 10% did not use branded terms (such as 'Thomson holiday' or 'EasyJet flights') at all during their online travel shopping experience. Importantly, over a third of travel buyers use a generic term as the last search before they purchase. Consumers change the type of keywords used as they move along the path to purchase. Of all the consumers sampled that made a final purchase, 29% started with a non-branded search term but ended with a brand search term.

This example illustrates perfectly how the purchase process is profoundly influenced by the success of search facilities and users' ability to refine searching over several visits – sometimes to competitors – before making a decision to use a particular supplier. E-shoppers do not need to go far before possibly being influenced to buy or shop elsewhere, raising the possibility that once they have changed habit they may not come back. To an extent this explains the ability of e-retailers such as Play and asos in the UK to take sales from more traditional outlets.

Product information

Having searched and browsed a site, visitors start to investigate further and require more information. The decision whether to make a product purchase is influenced by the information made available once a product has been successfully identified. There is an interaction between the price/promotion/ photographic representation/information made available to the e-shopper and whether there is sufficient information to make a purchase.

From commencement, the principles remain the same whereby e-shoppers require:

- clear product information
- clear pricing
- good images, with ability to increase size or view detail where possible
- added-value features such as product reviews, particularly independent ones
- stock availability
- clear purchasing instructions
- clear delivery pricing and timescales.

As recently as 2002, many sites with a large product portfolio showed 'no image available' for a selection of products, but quickly realized that this led to shopper dissatisfaction and so improved product presentation. Sites that provided details on stock availability at the 'found' stage were rated highly as e-shoppers became frustrated with sites that promoted items that were subsequently found to be out of stock after progressing through the checkout procedure – or even contacted following order placement.

In 2007 we see that the introduction of video streaming, 3D viewing and product manipulation have improved consumer perspectives and confidence in what they are buying and their provision increases the rate of customer sales conversion. Successful 'new' UK sites such as asos (sales up 86% year on year 2006–7) use catwalk video as well as static 3D images with zoom functionality to show fashion items in use, driving up the propensity of the shopper to purchase.

Shopping basket

Once a decision is made 'maybe' to buy, sites offer a 'basket' or 'trolley' in which to place prospective purchases. Multi-currency shopping baskets were relatively common on multinational sites in 2000 but these were widely disliked (introducing a degree of confusion into the purchasing decision) and soon became local currency oriented. By mid-2002, surveys were suggesting that traditional retailers (Argos, Kays, John Lewis) had caught up with the 'dotcoms' (Amazon, bol, crocus) in terms of shopping basket functionality.

Standards, and therefore expectations, were set requiring:

- clear product descriptions
- pictures reinforcing description
- easy removal, amendment or addition
- clear navigation back to similar products/home/new search as required
- clear navigation to basket at any stage of the shop
- ability to save and return to products in the future – used as wish list
- clear delivery pricing and information.

Checkout

As with standard store visits, there is a need to check out and pay for the goods ordered and once again a series of good practice rules are demanded by shoppers who frequent those sites that provide them. A clear summary of what is being purchased, including delivery details and pricing, is required, but most of all e-shoppers need firm and readily identifiable security of payment reassurances. They soon learned the new language of online security – urls beginning with 'https' and new logos of 'Verisign' and 'Thwaite' who provide online secure certificates. Yellow padlocks have become a must if a site is to be trusted with payment and personal details. Initially, credit details were often retained but when given the option e-shoppers prefer to provide these each time. Clearly most visitors to an information resource or service are not parting with their money (although this might change as pay as you view continues to increase) but there are important lessons here for information professionals.

Registration or application needs to be as simple and quick as possible with information only being asked for if absolutely necessary for the transaction. Any feature that could speed up the process brings dividends to online providers. Postcode searches (accurate ones), alternative delivery addresses, not having to repeat common information (log-in and user accounts) all help the process and encourage repeat visits. Requests for 'irrelevant' information in the eyes of the e-shopper – such as birth dates – are frowned upon ('they do not ask me this in a store' is a typical riposte). No additional or surprise costs nor presumption of opt-ins are wanted – but are often received – and e-shoppers are increasingly wary of giving details that might lead to the spam that is invading and clogging their e-mail inboxes.

Order tracking

Once an order has been placed there is a new requirement for order tracking, a further information need. The 'pure play' online retailers do not want customer contact – it adversely affects transaction cost. E-shoppers want to know what is happening and they are given the means to find out for themselves. Good practice demands regular e-mail updates and the ability to track order progress – stock, picking, despatch. Ability to contact a help facility if there turn out to be problems is also welcomed.

E-shopper behavioural patterns

E-shoppers have been surprisingly consistent in their behaviour over time except for the fact that as confidence grows they go to sites more often with the intention of making more purchases than they did before. However, research suggests that some 25% of all visitors are researching purchases that will be made in more traditional ways (eDigitalResearch, May 2007). This shows the information-pulling power of the internet and the fact that it is continuing to have a greater effect than just the delivery of direct sales.

We shall learn later how digital information consumers bounce around the virtual space looking for what they want. This is true also of e-shoppers. They 'research' many sites, purchase on a few trusted ones when the price and package is correct and cross-check by dipping into high-street stores to check that the deal is correct.

E-shopping visit patterns (Figure 3.6) remain fairly constant – with a peak on Monday lunchtimes and early evenings (very similar to that of the virtual scholar). E-shoppers will research products prior to purchase online and then purchase at a store (offline) or vice versa. This occurs after a weekend of

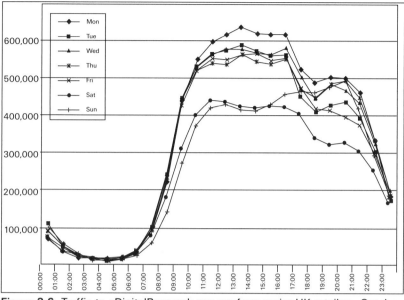

Figure 3.6 Traffic to eDigitalResearch servers from major UK retailers, October 2007

research or store visits when products can be seen and identified prior to price comparison and search without recourse to a store re-visit.

Looking at the usage and buying patterns for Christmas 2006 and 2007 in the UK (Table 3.2) provides further proof of the e-shopper's embrace of the new digital world and the re-ordering of time-honoured activities. Online Christmas and 'Sales' shopping profoundly affected the entire retail sector for the first time in 2007. While traditional retailers, unnerved by the effects of a credit crunch and overcapacity, went on early disaster-avoidance 'Sale', e-retailers, facing huge demand and under-supply, tuned their prices in real time against availability and requirement data to maximize profitability.

Table 3.2 Sales and spend, Christmas 2006 v. 2007

December 2007	Traffic v. 2006	People spending	Spend v. 2006	Spend £
Peak Sales Day Mon 10th	+ 6%	5.3m	+106%	£370m
Christmas Day 25th	+30.3%	4.4m	+169%	£ 83.85m
Boxing Day 26th	+38.6%	7.46m	+ 32%	£41m
December 27th	+13.6%	7.39m	N/A	N/A
Month of December	+11.6%	23.45m	+ 49.5%	£ 5.41m

Traffic (the number of unique visitors visiting a website) during December 2007 was 11.6% higher than December 2006, however the number of users purchasing was up by 50%. Whilst in previous years many had looked and researched at Christmas, here was proof that if the offer was right they would buy as well.

Of course the web is forever on and this is beginning to tell. Thus, following the lead of US traders in 2006, several leading retailers – as always looking for that extra shilling, including Marks & Spencer, Dixons and Comet – ran online sales promotions on Christmas Day itself, attracting significant levels of business whilst high-street shops were shut. Table 3.2 shows that site traffic peaked earlier on Christmas Day. From this data it is estimated that 4.4 million people bought goods online on Christmas Day 2007 and spent a total of £84 million, which was 169% more than 2006. The spend on Christmas Day 2007 was more than double (+104.5%) the £41 million recorded for Boxing Day (IMRG, 2008).

New buying patterns and habits continue to emerge from the new digital world, sometimes replicating habits formed from the traditional high street. One leading UK retailer (DeVere Forster, Director, Dixons.co.uk) commented in January 2008:

> In the period before Christmas we noticed a new phenomenon in buying patterns, which we called 'e-camping'. Thousands of keen buyers engaged in 'e-camping', mimicking the tradition of camping outside bricks and mortar stores, signing up for e-mail alerts to secure products with limited supply, such as the Nintendo Wii, as new stock arrived on our site. Traditional British behavioural patterns don't apply online – the door to our store is wide open and the customers who secure the stock are the ones who manage to click their mice milliseconds more quickly than their virtual queuing neighbours.
>
> (Austin, 2008)

New brands and new opportunities

There has been a change in consumer choice of outlets, with new brands quickly establishing themselves. 'Pure play' outlets became household names in a short time and leaders in site innovation, customer service and most of all pricing. Bezo's Amazon.com became a worldwide success and sites such as jungle.com, streetsonline, figleaves and, more recently, Play and asos, have gained significant retail market share in the UK. The internet has provided an opportunity for local organizations to 'think global' and yet still compete on a relatively level basis.

Increasing consumer use of 'price comparison' sites to buy branded goods and services such as insurance and financial products has meant that any kind of traditional regional pricing or outlet differential pricing has been made more difficult. It has also allowed local stores to compete and build reputation by increasing use of independent customer reviews and testimonials to help build trust and confidence in new brands and unrecognized/untried organizations. This has reduced the costs required for market entry, and the ability to market to a wider geographic audience quickly and easily has provided an invitation to both entrepreneurial spirit and investment cash to grow profitable new businesses – albeit now with a more circumspect view than that seen in the heady days of the dot.com boom.

Traditional organizations have watched a greater share of sales being carried out online and gradually have begun to invest in appropriate technology. A number purchased ailing dot.com boomers at a vastly reduced valuation than during the dot.com boom (e.g. Argos and jungle, Woolworths and streetsonline). Others have recognized the building consumer demand and started to build robust systems and support to grow their online presence, e.g. Comet Electrical, John Lewis, Tesco.

This 'revolution' has not been confined to retailers of goods and services. Other markets have started to see shifts in consumer research and purchasing behaviour.

The growth of transactional auction sites, particularly eBay, has had a profound effect on the online shopper demographic in both the US and UK. The presence of a central location to buy and sell all kinds of items on a level playing field and to meet other users with similar interests, provides a powerful marketplace for the sale of goods and services by a passionate community of individuals and small businesses. By 2007 eBay had a global presence in 37 markets, including the US, and had an astonishing 233 million registered users worldwide. In the UK it was calculated in February 2006 that more than 68,000 people were earning their primary or secondary income from the site. By March 2007 in the UK every other internet user (47%) visited eBay.co.uk at least once a month and the site reached an audience of just under 15 million users (eBay, 2008). Users from lower-income brackets and socio-economic groups found a simple financial outlet to spend and generate income. Through this, the internet has become more accessible and desirable – the e-shopper habit has spread accordingly.

As a reflection of these changes, the top 20 e-retail online sellers site list for 2007 in the UK showed a mix of traditional and 'pure play' organizations (Table 3.3).

Rank	Organization	Site URL

Table 3.3 UK Top 20 e-retail websites, October 2007
(Source: IMRG)

Rank	Organization	Site URL
1	Amazon UK	www.amazon.co.uk
2	Play.com	www.play.com
3	Argos	www.argos.co.uk
4	Tesco.com	www.tesco.com
5	Apple Computer	www.apple.com
6	Dell EMEA	www.euro.dell.com
7	Amazon.com	www.amazon.com
8	Marks & Spencer	www.marksandspencer.com
9	Tesco Direct	www.direct.tesco.com
10	Next	www.next.co.uk
11	HMV.co.uk	www.hmv.co.uk
12	Expedia.co.uk	www.expedia.co.uk
13	Thomson Holidays	www.thomson.co.uk
14	lastminute.com	www.lastminute.com
15	Currys	www.currys.co.uk
16	Ticketmaster UK	www.ticketmaster.co.uk
17	John Lewis	www.johnlewis.com
18	Ryanair	www.ryanair.com
19	easyJet	www.easyjet.co.uk
20	British Airways	www.britishairways.com

The IMRG-Hitwise Hot Shops List of the top 50 UK e-retailers is the key indicator of online merchant performance. The List is published quarterly and tracks popularity, as indicated by visits, of those selling goods and services within the IMRG Capgemini Index Classification. This List is based on October 2007 data. The IMRG-Hitwise Hot Shops List excludes eBay and price comparison/aggregator websites such as Kelkoo and Google Product Search.

Traditionally, high-street retailers have received less online traffic than their pure play online competitors, except during the Christmas and January Sale periods. Analysis based on two Hitwise custom categories consisting of the top 50 high-street retailers and the top 50 pure play retailers in the UK (excluding online auctions and ticket retailers) revealed that, in 2006, high-street retailers only overtook their online rivals during the peak month of December, but in 2007 they overtook them in September and continued to widen the gap. This provides further evidence that shoppers' behaviour has had a profound effect on traditional retailers and that they have recognized the challenge and opportunity of e-commerce (IMRG, 2008).

In addition, the travel industry has also seen a shift in consumer behaviour allowing research and purchases to be conducted online without resort to traditional high-street travel agents using paper-based brochures.

Another more recent phenomenon, the social network site, particularly amongst the under 25s in the UK, shows the speed with which such an interactive medium can assist consumers to change their behaviour. An example is Facebook (one of three major social network sites) that was founded in 2004. By the end of that year it had 1 million users and by October 2007 this had grown to 59 million active global users. Almost half (48%) of Britons online (15.3 million people) visited at least one of the ten most popular social networks in August 2007. In addition, three of the ten fastest growing social network brands are formed around specific interest groups – business, travel and music (NetRatings, 2007).

This adds another dimension to our research and product seeking e-shopper. In September 2006, www.facebook.com was the 126th most visited url in the UK, but its market share increased thirtyfold over the next 12 months, from 0.056% of all UK internet visits to 1.66% in September 2007. It became the fifth most visited url in the UK, and was also the fifth most popular source of traffic for other websites. In the retail sector, www.facebook.com refers 1% of UK internet traffic to shopping and classifieds websites.

In September 2007, 3.1% of UK internet visits to the Hitwise Shopping and Classifieds category came from a Hitwise custom category consisting of the top 25 social networks in the UK. Auctions, clothing and entertainment are the main retail beneficiaries of social networking traffic as consumers exercise word-of-mouth influence on research and purchase habits. The question is where e-shoppers lead, will information-seekers follow? The British Library thinks so and so do a good few university libraries.

In fact online auction sites, in particular eBay, are the main retail beneficiaries of the social networking phenomenon, receiving 31.4% of all downstream traffic that social networks send to shopping and classifieds sites. The more traditional retail categories – department stores and apparel and accessories sites – come next, respectively receiving 1 in 8 and 1 in 9 of all UK retail visits from social networks. The close links between social networks and the entertainment industry help music and video and games retailers, which are the fourth and fifth biggest beneficiaries respectively. Combined, these five categories account for 72% of all online retail traffic sent from social networks (IMRG, 2007b).

This also gives our newly empowered e-shopper an enhanced voice, not only using word of mouth to inform friends, family and colleagues but also providing the ability to complain and discuss in open forum issues regarding an organization's goods and services. Blogs and forums are being specifically set up for users to bring together consumers with common cause; the same thing is now beginning to happen in the digital information world.

e-resistance

It is worthwhile noting at this point that not all consumers have accepted this behavioural shift. There are some who remain reluctant to embrace change. Apart from age there continue to be issues with security of online transactions and, in the case of buying goods, the need to 'touch, feel and even smell' products. There is of course the social aspect of 'shopping' that should not be discounted. E-shoppers use the internet as just another channel to interact with organizations, depending on their particular needs at the time. Research conducted into why some internet users did not purchase any Christmas presents online in 2007 is revealing: 69% did not do so because they 'enjoyed shopping offline', while 18% did not have a credit card and 10% did not trust security on sites.

Technology driving change

Major shifts have been noted in consumer behaviour as technology ushers in change and allows organizations to develop and offer new products facilitated by the new medium. Both the availability and quality of access to the internet has continued to grow and has become more the norm in a household than not. The 'pay-as-you-use' model of slow 'dial up' connections has given way to the availability of 'always on' broadband access with competition driving down costs of access. In 2007, of all UK households including Northern Ireland, over 15 million (61%) had access to the internet. This was an increase of nearly 1 million households (7%) since 2006. The regions with the highest level of access were the South West and London, both with 69%. The regions with the lowest access levels were Yorkshire and the Humber, the North East and Northern Ireland, each with 52%. Of UK households with internet access, 84% had a broadband connection in 2007, up from 69% in 2006. As in 2006, London had the highest level of households with broadband internet access at 60%. Of London households with internet access, 88% had a broadband connection (National Statistics, 2007a).

Finding on the internet

Being able to find products and services efficiently is another key factor in the growth of internet use. The Google mission of founders Larry Page and Sergey Brin in 1996 was to organize the world's information and make it universally accessible and useful. They hypothesized that a search engine that analysed the relationships between websites would produce better ranking of results than the existing techniques of that time, which ranked results according to the number of times the search term appeared on a page. Finally launched in 1998, the word quickly spread to information seekers around the globe.

Google quickly became recognized as the world's largest search engine and it has become one of the top five visited sites in the world with 81.9 million global users per month. It rapidly became the number one search engine in the UK as well as in Germany, France, Italy, Netherlands, Spain, Switzerland and Australia (Nielsen//NetRatings, 2007).

The ability efficiently to find what they are looking for using multiple words and phrases further empowers consumers but also raises expectations for any other sites they are using (whatever the sector – academic, government or commercial). The 'Google-ization' of search has led to dissatisfaction with a site's search functionality – something that continues into 2008.

For most e-commerce sites in the UK some 25–33% of visits are generated from search engines whilst Google's market share in 2007 in the USA was 64% (+10% v. 2006) and 79% (+4%) in the UK (IMRG, 2007a). Google has a dominant position in the search market and an essential influence in the growth of efficient use of the internet.

Product offer

Meanwhile fundamental market shifts in consumer behaviour have been driven by the use of the internet to reduce transaction and distribution costs and provide significantly lower cost alternatives to traditional purchasing methods. An example has been seen in the UK travel industry. 'Low frill' airlines such as EasyJet and Ryanair have used demand modelling, effective asset use and internet access (reduced distribution costs, ticketless travel, paperless operations) to drive down cost. Hotels and other elements of travel such as car hire, parking, insurance have followed suit and carry out transactions directly through 'portals' (web doors). This in turn has allowed consumers to become informed travellers – their own travel agent – and spawned another industry of 'word of mouth' recommendation (or otherwise) from fellow travellers, e.g. tripadvisor.co.uk. This has lead to an unprecedented increase in UK consumers visiting European destinations – for both short and longer visits. Travel within Europe has become inexpensive, accessible and desirable – and weekends away more common and workforces more mobile.

Another example is Apple's iTunes which, following rights deals with all major record companies, racked up $70m sales in its first 12 months and effectively fatally wounded the traditional music distribution channels. In August 2007 Apple announced that sales at its online music store iTunes had topped three billion songs. The company, which makes the iPod digital media player, revealed that over one billion tracks had been sold in the last six months. The iTunes online store features a catalogue of over five million songs, 550 television shows and 500 movies. The service launched in April 2003 and reached the one billion milestone of tracks sold in February 2006.

These technological examples illustrate not only a previously unknown pace of change but also a paradigm shift in consumer behaviour that is also having a profound effect on businesses and how they approach their consumers. It has led to the concept of the 'multi-channel customer' much talked about by organizations. This is a fundamentally flawed concept when viewed from the user point of view since e-shoppers regard themselves as 'cross-channel' and use whichever channel is convenient and available at the time – not necessarily the cheapest; a message that has still not got across to digital information providers.

Take the example of a terminally expired washing machine at my home. If it is Monday and my three teenage children are coming home from University for the coming weekend then I have no problem in going onto the internet, finding the right product, price and acceptable delivery and fitting options, and placing an order. If it is the Friday before they are coming home then it is more of an issue and my purchase decision will be based on immediate availability, pick up (collect at store facility?) and the size of vehicle that I have available. I may even then consider the local plumber as well. In this exercise I may have used all the channels available to me without much thought and would expect a uniform approach from the suppliers. Then they all change their plans . . . and I go back to plan A!

The 'cross-channel' e-shopper operates under the same rules – changing channel as emotional and physical requirements dictate. Organizations have to be adaptable and offer a single face to this challenge – one that in 2008 is still not being met in all cases.

The knock-on effect of the growth of e-shopping

While it is relatively easy to understand the change retailers and other sites are being forced to make to meet this consumer behavioural shift, it is worth noting the knock-on effect for other industries. New industries have been created around these new consumer demands. Apart from the obvious requirement for supply and servicing of hardware and software there is now a requirement to maximize how sites interact with their users. With more investment in consumer interfaces (the website), and therefore on the importance of the return on investment (ROI) from sites and associated support, there has been a growing focus on the customer experience to maximize conversion (number of purchasers v. number of unique site visitors).

Usability

One example of such a new industry is 'usability'. Defined as 'the ease with which visitors are able to use a website', website usability is not just about making sure everything on the site works. It looks at speed of use (not necessarily speed of page loading), navigation – searching and finding products, and ease of use – how quickly and easily visitors are able to make use of the site, how quickly they could make a purchase, e.g. Amazon one-click.

The need for website usability has perhaps been best expressed by usability 'guru' Jakob Nielsen's Law of the Internet User Experience: 'Users spend most of their time on other sites' (Nielsen, n.d.). Usability has become a concern for e-commerce organizations because of its potential impact, positive or negative, on return on investment. Consumers now contrast and compare their experiences of websites in one sector with other sectors, once again blurring previously existing traditional boundaries – e.g. retail shopping v. buying of financial products v. obtaining scholarly information.

In addition the use of web analytic tools and automated tagging of site visitors allow monitoring of site page views, unique visitors and customer 'journeys'. Most importantly key customer 'drop off' points can be monitored to find where potential users may be experiencing issues with site usage. This is another lesson that information providers need to learn.

Customer satisfaction monitoring and market research is easier, faster and less expensive than it is in traditional purchasing and it is leading to major organizations implementing comprehensive feedback and monitoring processes. Independent product reviews (introduced by Amazon as early as 1996) became another power shift towards the consumer.

If consumer influence and behaviour shape the way sites are being designed and constructed (the drive to understand the key shopper journeys) so did the seismic shift in the 'back end' logistics required to support it. Thus the growth in e-retail sales is directly linked to the number of parcels and therefore support logistics required. It is estimated that 540 million e-shopper-related parcels were delivered in 2006 in the UK. This grew to 860 million in 2007 – an increase of 59%. Expectations change quickly. To make internet sales work in the mind of the consumer, delivery time-scales have to be acceptable. Previously, catalogue-based organizations had always quoted 28 days for direct delivery. Pure play online retailers quoted 3–5 day delivery and offered next-day as well. The 'pick, pack and deliver' process had to be fast and efficient and it was. E-retailers understood this and demanded more of their delivery partners. The returns and refund process had to be similarly slick to build consumer confidence in the process. Pure play online retailers made this work in their favour (e.g. figleaves) with e-mail communication used to quickly confirm the processes and credit refunds to appropriate credit cards. In the late 1990s and early 2000s some high-street retailers struggled with these processes, stores not accepting products bought on the internet sometimes setting up systems with different product codes for the same products between stores, catalogues and website. This improved as organizations understood the advantage of users being able to return items to bricks and mortar stores as well as via post or carrier – but it took time.

Challenges in the grocery market

A further example of these logistical challenges can be found in the grocery market in the UK. In the late 1990s the UK's major grocer, Tesco, stole a march on its rivals and launched an online grocery store based on the principle of a local store pick – no central warehouse – with less burdensome investment therefore than that which had brought down pure play rivals in the USA such as Webvan. By 2000 Tesco were reporting sales of £125 million and 250,000 registered users. By 2007 their reported online sales during the year reached a record-breaking £1.226 billion with over

850,000 regular online grocery customers placing 250,000 orders a week.

In November 2007, Sainsbury's (the UK's second largest grocer) released interim figures which revealed that its online home delivery sales had increased by more than 40% so far that year. The supermarket chain reported that it was receiving 80,000 orders each week via its website and its online home delivery service. The total number of Sainsbury's stores (they had switched from a central distribution system) offering the service had increased to 137 during the same year. The supermarket chain reports that by March 2010 it expects to expand the service to 200 stores and more than double its online sales.

Each of these orders has to be supported with pick, pack and delivery – in Tesco's and Sainsbury's case from physical outlets, namely the local supermarket. The grocers, led by rival Ocado, introduced one-hour delivery time-slots. E-shoppers' expectations are that all e-retailers should be able to do the same and have started demanding similar time-slots from all retailers. e-shoppers will continue to demand changes in delivery methodologies to encourage better use of technology to make delivery more efficient and less time-consuming. Organizations will need to cope with changing communication needs and become more efficient in organizing their support.

Customer contact

The internet created another challenge for organizations – e-mail. Telephone traffic had already been identified, largely understood and managed but the invention of electronic mail offered a new challenge, particularly as internet users quickly saw it as a medium of choice – no waiting for answers from complex telephone answering systems plus an automated record of communication.

Some organizations handled it well – particularly the pure play retailers who saw it as their medium of choice as well (if they had to communicate at all). Unfortunately this was not universal and some organizations continue to struggle to achieve consumer expectation in this regard – Figure 3.7 shows that 69% of all internet users expect a reply to an e-mail within 24 hours. The

Table 3.4 E-mail performance of UK online retailers 2000-7 (%)
(Source: eDigitalResearch UK site research 2000-7)

	48 hours+	24-48 hours	12-24 hours	6-12 hours	Under 6 hours
2000	30	29	14	19	8
2001	25	15	23	16	21
2002	27	13	22	14	25
2003	28	13	24	13	23
2004	36	15	22	9	18
2005	36	11	22	8	23
2006	43	9	14	8	23
2007	46	12	14	6	19

research suggests that over half do not get a reply in this time (eDigitalResearch, Dec 2007). Table 3.4 shows e-mail performance from a mix of retailers in 2000–7.

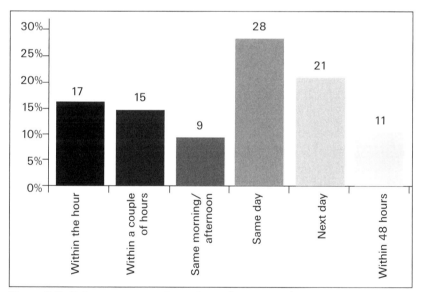

Figure 3.7 E-shopper expectations of e-mail response times

The future of the e-shopper?

The availability of faster, 'always on' internet speeds will continue to fuel consumer change. Technological changes, including the convergence of the traditional 'boxes' of TV and computers and 'nano' technological advances (allowing even smaller devices to complete even bigger tasks), will continue to drive change in behaviour patterns. There will be new entrants into marketplaces and reorganization of existing players to cope with changing consumer behaviour.

Organizations that have invested in 'bricks and mortar' traditional shopping outlets will encourage cross-channel consumerism while seeking continually to reduce transaction costs and encourage acquisition and retention of loyal customers. Pure play retailers and smaller niche-based outlets will continue to pick away at the traditional retailer base with improved products, competitive pricing (by driving down transaction costs and with lower operational overheads) and delivery of efficient logistics and customer-service support.

Improved identification of site visitors will allow sophisticated personalization of content. Pricing and product offers will be based on past consumption and product viewing patterns. Sophisticated segmentation algorithms will provide e-shoppers with refined choice and more information to allow informed decision making – and more opportunities to buy! They will continue to embrace this enthusiastically whilst demanding best practice standards across all providers in all marketplaces.

While some technological advances and changes are predictable now – for example, webcams in houses for sale, selected streaming entertainment on demand (personalized with regard to other programmes, films, music consumed before), immediate news feeds and product information – others are not. Organizations will remain under constant scrutiny and will be required to monitor and react quickly to consumer demand and change.

What is certain is that consumers have become newly empowered in the last 12 years. They have discovered the fact that the internet gives them the ability to research products and services and tell each other (like-minded individuals whom they do not necessarily know) what is good and what is bad. Most of all they have found the confidence to become e-shoppers in growing numbers and to embrace change and technological advancement.

Following Christmas 2007, internet users were asked whether, based on their experience (of purchasing Christmas gifts), they would be ordering more, less or the same next year; 'the same' reported 50.2%, 'more' reported 44.9% (eDigitalResearch, Jan 2008).

The Google Generation has found financial stability and real purchasing power. The e-shopper story will fast-forward.

Conclusions

We have seen that the rapid rise of the e-shopper has had a growing significance for the e-commerce economy. This influence, however, is more far-reaching than that. As organizations develop strategies and features to convert their site visitors to site customers (buyers), these same internet users will have common expectations across all sectors: from ease of finding products with efficient and common search methodologies, secure payments, easy-to-use registration and application forms, information downloads, availability of products on demand, to multiple and new devices as technology develops. These users will use the same influencers to make decisions about visiting information providers – whether they are social network sites or independent reviews – *and* will continue to demand new standards in traditional methods of information provision.

Notes

1   For an excellent time line of the early history of the world wide web see Cailliau (1995).

2   Interactive Media in Retail Group (IMRG, www.imrg.org) is a membership group that promotes e-retail in the UK. Retail members contribute sales figures to produce an index of online sales. As well as providing information and market intelligence, the IMRG promotes best practice and industry standards, and IMRG's Information and Market Intelligence. IMRG Index Classification: Beer/wine/spirits; Books; CDs/tapes/records; Clothing/footwear/accessories; Computer hardware/peripherals/consumables;

Consumer electronics; Digital downloads (e.g. music, software); Flowers; Food, beverages and household supplies; Furniture; Garden/DIY; Health and beauty; Home appliances (e.g. washing machines); Household goods (e.g. kitchenware, bedding); Jewellery/watches; Software; Sporting goods; Tickets (e.g. cinema, theatre, events); Toys; Travel (e.g. flights, holidays, hotels, car hire); Videogames; Videos/DVDs.

References

Austin, M. (2008) *Happy e-Campers*, www.internetretailing.net/news/happy-e-campers.

Cailliau, R. (1995) *A Short History of the Web: text of a speech delivered at the launching of the European branch of the W3 Consortium*, Paris, (2 November), www.netvalley.com/archives/mirrors/robert_cailliau_speech.htm.

ComScore (2007) *comScore and Google UK Reveal Importance of Search Engines at all Stages of Path to Purchase in Travel Sector*, press release, (10 January), www.comscore.com/press/release.asp?press=1991.

eBay (2008) eBay – The World's Online Marketplace, http://pages.ebay.co.uk/aboutebay/thecompany/companyoverview.html.

IMRG (2007a) *Hitwise*, (April).

IMRG (2007b) *Hitwise UK Retail and Social Networking Update*, (October).

IMRG (2008) *Hitwise UK Retail Update:post-Christmas 2007 analysis*, (January).

Johnson, C. (2005) US *eCommerce 2005 to 2010: a five-year forecast and analysis of US online retail sales*, Forrester.

National Statistics (2007a) Omnibus Survey: Northern Ireland Omnibus Survey, survey of internet service providers, www.statistics.gov.uk/CCI/nugget.asp?ID=8.

National Statistics (2007b) Omnibus Survey: Office for National Statistics, www.statistics.gov.uk/cci/nugget.asp?id=1711

NetRatings (2007) *Facebook is now the UK's Most Popular Social Network*, www.nielsen-netratings.com/pr/pr_070925_UK.pdf.

Nielsen//NetRatings (2007) 6/03 and 6/04.

Nielsen, J. (n.d.) www.useit.com/alertbox/9605.html (item 8).

Wikipedia (2008) *E-commerce*, http://en.wikipedia.org/wiki/E-commerce.

The library in the digital age

MICHAEL MOSS

Summary

It is time for the information professions in the UK that lag behind their peers in North America, Australasia and even sub-Saharan Africa to wake up to the realities of what might be described as the second digital revolution that is rapidly being colonized by other disciplines with theory and rhetoric that address its far-reaching implications for the way we live and do business. A great deal is written about the library in the digital age, largely from the perspective of technology that is often characterized as 'new' or 'emerging' with 'exciting' possibilities, with little regard for the way knowledge production, categorization, management, distribution and consumption are being transformed. Such introspective hyperbole, which often gives the impression of clutching at straws, ignores previous information revolutions, such as the development of printing in 15th-century Europe, and, perhaps more importantly, the long preoccupation with information and its adjuncts in European thought, stretching back to classical times.

This chapter explores the relationship between this considerable body of knowledge and information provision and discovery that speaks directly to this second digital revolution. It argues that there is an implicit false binary opposition in much of the discussion between the semantic and the technical that unhelpfully sets traditionalists against innovators. It warns against techno-determinism, but also a nostalgia for an ordered past and a retreat into curatorial gulags. It suggests that an 'archival paradigm' might more accurately reflect the ontology of digital content that itself predicates a convergence in professional practice among archivists, librarians and museum curators. The chapter concludes from this perspective, that the information community needs to return to what it is good at, 'collection development', leaving resource discovery to the search engines and internet providers. Emphatically it must work with rather than against societal expectations and practice. It must stop thinking it knows best, otherwise it will be in danger of becoming irrelevant.

Context

> She was intensely conventional and when she had started to read she thought perhaps she ought to do some of it at least in the place set aside for the purpose, namely the palace library. But though it was called the library and was indeed lined with books, a book was seldom if ever read there.
>
> (Bennett, 2007, 19)

In Buckingham Palace library, according to Alan Bennett, 'ultimatums were delivered . . . , lines drawn, prayer books compiled and marriages decided upon'; whereas elsewhere libraries are becoming homes to serried ranks of computer terminals and readers are ceasing to want to read books but instead to discover the resources they need online by using search engines with global reach, especially Google. If they have broadband at home, they no longer need to visit the library, but instead either use it as a 'switching centre' to access its subscription services, or more commonly bypass it altogether by accessing content directly from providers in a way that lacks the inter-mediation familiar in the print culture (Atkinson, 1990). Alan Bennett's novel *An Uncommon Reader* opens with the Queen accidentally discovering the Westminster council's mobile library in the palace yard; whereas increasingly local authorities are being encouraged to scrap their mobile libraries and deliver 'learning materials' over the internet through The People's Network (Mathieson, 2004). This trend makes 'what was familiar appear strange and what was natural seem arbitrary' (Burke, 2000, 2). We no longer consult an encyclopedia to find information, instead we Google and more likely than not we find what we think we want in Wikipedia, which prides itself on content that represents the 'wisdom of crowds' that Jaron Lanier condemns as 'digital Maoism' (Surowiecki, 2004; Lanier, 2006). Gertrude Himmelfarb warns 'But democratization of the access to knowledge should not be confused with the democratization of knowledge itself. And this is where the internet, or any system of electronic networking, may be misleading and even pernicious. In cyberspace, every source seems as authoritative as every other. As that child on TV put it, "lots of people" will profess to have the answer to his question' (Himmelfarb, 1999, 615). Jeanneney is concerned that the democratization itself is illusory and dependent on Google's 'uncertain' plan of classification that inevitably reflects an anglophone cultural imperialism (Jeanneney, 2006, 6).

These serious concerns may be why Mohsen Zuhran can describe the bizarre new Bibliotheca Alexandrina as a 'lighthouse of knowledge', even – 'If being a librarian once meant filing and retrieving books, it now means operating immensely complicated and expensive information systems, combining knowledge of traditional books and microfilm with that of computers, fibre-optic cables, server networks, elaborate software formats, audio-visual systems, among many other things' (Stille, 2002, 262). Its mission is 'To be a center of excellence for the production and dissemination of knowledge and to be a place of dialogue and understanding between cultures and peoples' (Bibliotheca Alexandrina, 2008). Gerald Grunberg, the senior consultant to the project, who previously worked on the new Bibliothèque nationale de France in Paris, justifies the conception – 'With globalization there is an enormous need for spaces where one will assemble and conserve the collective memory of a community or of a country. The more globalization we have, the more these sort of places are necessary. It is not a paradox' (Stille, 2002, 265). Bruce Winston from the School of Global Leadership and Enterprise at Regent University, Virginia, developed this line of thinking about the future of the library in the digital age suggesting they 'may look more like museums where one-of-a-kind archives are held, such as the Library of Congress. Patrons of the university library would spend time studying archives as one might do in a museum, but the traditional book would be available by electronic access' (Beaudoin, 2006, 280). In a sense this takes us back to the *wunderkammer* of the enlightenment that was filled with undifferentiated objects brought together by the collector.

This is a profoundly different conception of the function of the library than in the past where it was considered a place of useful knowledge, self improvement and reflection. Inscribed above the portals of the 2500 libraries in the USA and UK founded by the steel magnate and philanthropist Andrew Carnegie between 1883 and 1919 was the legend 'Let there be light', made manifest through open stacks where readers could browse and learn as it were serendipitously. In Grunberg's vision the light may not burn less brightly, but the function of the library is no longer 'open access' but to serve as a secure repository, akin, as Winston suggests, to an archive or a museum. Such a vision makes the assumptions that libraries as institutions will not even have a role as 'switching centres' in the supply chain for digital assets and that 'collective memory' and cultural dialogue can be readily translated into collecting policies. Winston proposed a radical view where the publishing industry effectively takes control of the supply not just of knowledge but of education itself (Beaudoin, 2006, 283). There is evidence that this is already happening, both formally through the publishing industry – for example in McGraw-Hill's 'specific-topical-documents' service, and to a much greater extent through informal provision that mostly lacks the mediation familiar in the analogue print culture and simply bypasses the academy. This conclusion is more than confirmed by the observation of Nicholas and his colleagues in CIBER in Chapter 6 where they argue that the consumer is moving closer to the publisher or distributor and away from the library as a provider. With such a shift and the advent of e-books the library may even cease to have a function as a repository in a conventional sense. Winston, however, also envisages the continuing need for a library as an *agora* or meeting place, a kind of permanent conference that can find expression in a shift in design away from 'collection oriented' architecture towards 'social oriented', 'service oriented' and 'customer oriented' architecture and interiors (Berndtson,

2006). As Berndtson puts it – 'The social aspect of libraries may be more important than we realize. More than ever, we need places where people can meet' (Berndtson, 2002, 7). Coates, reflecting on the library of 20 years ago, comments – 'Even if libraries were slightly dull they were a family and community institution playing an essential role in lifelong learning, social cohesion and pleasurable reading' (Coates, 2005).

The library as social space or space for reflection?

Such a redefinition of the library as a social space is not without its critics. As long ago as 1997 Sally Tisdale in an article in *Harper's Magazine* complained that 'her beloved library had been turned into an Alice's Restaurant of infotainment options: a library in which reverence had succumbed to relevance, an honourable atmosphere of quiet had declined into pure noise, and the hallowed experience of focused reading had been replaced by ubiquitous videoscreens and Net Nuts' (Wisner, 2000, 14). During the following decade such experience became a commonplace – 'Computers were introduced to libraries and book collections were allowed to fall into neglect. As a consequence, demand dwindled. Libraries found a role instead as free internet cafes' (Brabazon, 2007a, 38, quoting in part Coates, 2005). Tara Brabazon flatly rejects such a reconfiguration of the library – 'Libraries are not internet cafes. They are places to not only find books, but to discover a way of ordering and organizing knowledge' (Brabazon, 2007a, 38). Their emphasis on spaces for reflection and contemplation is echoed by David Levy, himself one of the inventors of the PC:

> For some of us, books and libraries symbolize some of the very qualities and modes of being that are threatened in our fast-paced instrumented lives. Books speak of time and depth and attention. They speak of a slower rhythm of life. And in their weighty physicality, they draw us back to our own materiality, and to the materiality of the world. Libraries are places not just where books can be found, but where people can temporarily remove themselves from the speed and busyness of life, where they can read and write and reflect. They are (or can be) shared sacred places in a secular, common world.   (Levy, 2001, 197)

Susan Greenfield, the neuroscientist, challenged her fellow peers in a debate in the United Kingdom House of Lords in 2005 to consider:

> When you read a book, the author usually takes you by the hand and you travel from the beginning to the middle to the end in a continuous narrative of interconnected steps. It may not be a journey with which you agree, or one that you enjoy, but none the less, as you turn the pages, one train of thought succeeds the last in a logical fashion. We can then compare one narrative with another and, in so doing, start to build up a conceptual framework that enables us to evaluate further journeys, which, in turn, will influence our individualised framework. We can place an isolated fact in a context that gives it a significance. So traditional education has enabled us to turn information into knowledge.
>
> Now imagine there is no robust conceptual framework. You are sitting in front of a multimedia presentation where you are unable, because you have not had the experience of many different intellectual journeys, to evaluate what is flashing up on the screen. The most immediate reaction would be to place a premium on the most obvious feature, the immediate sensory content, the 'yuk' and 'wow' factor.
>
> You would be having an experience rather than learning. The sounds and sights of a fast-moving multimedia presentation displace any time for reflection, or any idiosyncratic or imaginative connections we might make as we turn the pages, and then stare at a wall to reflect upon them.

She concluded not by sounding a retreat, but with a question:

> We have access to unlimited and up-to-date information at the touch of a button, but in this new, answer-rich world, surely we must ensure that we are able to pose appropriate, meaningful questions?
>
> (Greenfield, 2006)

At the heart of all these criticisms of the new information order is a cry for the space and time for reflection that does negate the idea of the library as a social space, just the sort of technology-rich learning space that we have chosen to make it (JISC, 2006). As Brabazon puts it 'Google has flattened expertise, creating confusion between finding information and possessing the literacy to evaluate and judge information . . . My fear is not of wiki or Google. My concern is that in the confusion between finding information and building knowledge, we lose not only the analogue objects and artefacts, but analogue ways of thinking . . . We have lost the capacity to value the particular, the unique, the ephemeral and the transitory' (Brabazon, 2007b). As Nicholas and his colleagues show in Chapter 6 her concerns are justified by the behaviour of users unfamiliar with analogue library practice or, perhaps more worryingly, going for 'quick wins' in scholarly discourse that is under increased pressure to justify itself but where there is as yet little empirical evidence to support such supposed gains.

Libraries as 'one-of-a-kind archives'

The restatement of the traditional role of the library as a warehouse of accumulated knowledge to be explored reflexively is not simply nostalgic. It resonates with Winston's idea of 'one-of-a-kind archives' that combines memory and reference. Memory, widely used to describe archives, libraries and museums, is a tricky concept which has attracted much debate that has served to complicate as much as to enlighten (Wood and Byatt, 2008). Great national libraries, such as the Prunksaal in the Hofburg in Vienna or the Library of Congress in Washington, represent the constructed and collective memory of nations that will inevitably reflect the concerns and pre-occupations of the present and their funders in much the same way as Google's algorithms do. This is true of every library and every website, however small, and should raise serious concerns when search engines have global reach. Such a conception of dominant discourses with their particular narratives and events was questioned after World War I in France by historians and thinkers, such as Febvre, Bloch and Braudel, who replaced a single national narrative with *histoire vraie* and challenged positivist perspectives by asserting that 'history was not "value free" and that historical facts were in reality "constructs" ' (Lucas, 1985, 4). The idea that *lieux de mémoire*, which for Pierre Nora included 'the archives and the tricolor;

libraries and festivals; dictionaries and the Pantheon; museums and the Arc de Triomphe; the Dictionnaire Larousse' and so on, were not only themselves constructs but also everything they contained served to destabilize them led to a re-examination of their purpose and function (Nora, 1996–8, 1, 6). The French philosopher Michel Foucault went further in unravelling the relationship between the dominant discourse and those that opposed it:

> Discourses are not once and for all subservient to power or raised up against it, any more than silences are. We must make allowance for the concept's complex and unstable process whereby discourse can be both an instrument and an effect of power, but also a hindrance, a stumbling block, a point of resistance and a starting point for an opposing strategy. Discourse transmits and produces power; it reinforces it, but also undermines and exposes it, renders it fragile and makes it possible to thwart it.
>
> (Foucault, 1990, 100–1)

The potential for the warehouse of knowledge to both legitimize and threaten authority concerned Jacques Derrida, who argued that: 'By incorporating the knowledge deployed in reference to it, the archive augments itself, engrosses itself, it gains in *auctoritas*. But in the same stroke it loses the absolute and meta-textual authority it might claim to have. One will never be able to objectivize it with no remainder. The archivist produces more archive, and that is why the archive is never closed. It opens out of the future' (Derrida, 1996, 67). From this perspective Jeanneney's railing against Google is not simply a francophone reaction to American imperialism, but a reasoned critique that embraces the 'other' in a European context where there is no common language (Jeanneney, 2006).

Although it is convenient to collapse the library, in the sense that it serves as a store of knowledge, into the archive, we must be careful about the use of terminology, even if archives and, for that matter, museums also claim to be memory institutions. There are precedents in antiquity for using the library to protect the canonical text of Greek tragedies (Casson, 2001), but this fiduciary function, as we shall see, is usually associated with the archive that has much in common with Levy's concept of the library as a 'shared sacred place' (Moss, 2006, 239). It may be that when content is increasingly represented by 1s and 0s and is delivered using the same distribution channel, there is little to differentiate archives, libraries and museums that just become different aspects of the one *wunderkammer*. Unlike books, which by definition exist in multiple copies, digital objects are unique and can be viewed and copied many times; but there is no guarantee that the surrogate copies are faithful renditions of the 'original' or phishing scams, just as there was no guarantee that texts copied in a monastic scriptorium were either faithful renditions of an original or simply forgeries (Clanchy, 1979). Defining digital objects as 'one-of-a-kind archives' is reinforced by and reinforces intellectual convergence that is predicated on notions that all information objects, whether analogue or digital, are 'texts' that can be read (Buckland, 1997).

In 1935 Walter Schuermeyer wrote: 'Nowadays one understands as a document any material basis for extending our knowledge which is available for study or comparison' (quoted in Buckland, 1997 and Schuermeyer, 1935, 537). This claim for the universality of text had its origins in the early 19th century with new approaches to hermeneutics, developed in the 20th century by Heidegger and Gadamer (Wolf and Buttman, 1807; Heidegger, 1962; Ormiston and Schrift, 1990; Malpas, 2005). They introduced notions of temporality into the understanding of texts – 'Time must be brought to light and genuinely grasped as the horizon of every understanding and interpretation' (Heidegger, 1978, 60). By so doing they rejected the concept of objective 'truths' and replaced it with the notion of subjective truths, conditioned by time and place. These ideas have become foundational to postmodern rhetoric that, as we have seen, challenges directly the 'modernist' episteme of the library (Dempsey, 2000; Glosiene and Manzhukh, 2005; Ray, 2001; Wisner, 2000). Paradoxically in postmodern thought, as Ron Day has pointed out, '"information" constitutes both its "inside" and its "outside"', as both knowledge and theory develop from information flows (Day, 1996). This is contested territory that drives some practitioners back into their curatorial gulags that at times lack intellectual credibility, let alone technical justification.

The library in the postmodern world

The attraction of convergence from a 'service oriented' perspective is that it appears to match user expectations for one-stop shopping for their inform-ation needs, and in a digital environment could be interpreted at best as breaking the link between physical space and the concept of archives, libraries, and museums. An access and service focus that is driven by technology ignores the curatorial actions required to select/appraise/privilege content for user communities. Some would deny even this has significance in the digital age, since for them the content of the internet as a whole constitutes one vast undifferentiated repository that can be explored freely using search engines that, according to Clifford Lynch, director of the Coalition for Networked Information in the United States, avoids 'the haphazard historical gerrymandering of knowledge into institutional collections belonging to communities' (Lynch, 2003). Such an attack on traditional curatorial practices plays to much postmodern thinking that assumes that since the evidence is problematic, then truth is unknowable and in our hip-hop world authenticity and veracity have no place. In 1994 Miksa predicted such a state of affairs, but was quick to observe 'the result appears to be something different than what is understood to be a library?' (Miksa and Doty, 1994). A techno-deterministic vision of this sort begs huge questions about the ontological status, quality and persistence of internet content, and the privileging mechanisms of search engines, such as Google, that are not easily resolved (Jeanneney, 2006). Brabazon is concerned that in addressing these questions we have become so 'marinated in the digital that we are in danger of losing analogue ways of thinking' (2007b).

It was in the analogue that Heidegger drew attention to the need to understand the ontology of objects, 'a knowing questioning of beings in their thatness and whatness' (Heidegger, 1978, 45), before we can begin to interpret them, which Gadamer later extended into a dialogic process (Malpas, 2005). Crucially Heidegger introduced the idea that apprehension of being necessarily involved in a 'relationship with and a relating to something' (Heidegger, 1978, 80; Day, 1994). In the library context such ontological preoccupations found expression in the documentalist school founded by Paul Otlet, whose *Traité de documentation: le livre sur le livre: théorie et pratique* of 1934 is the seminal text (Otlet, 1934). For Otlet, by questioning the 'thatness and whatness' of the book, it becomes possible to understand its role not only 'in representing and embodying truth', but, through its relationships, the way it has 'acted as a metaphor for the organization of larger social practices and spaces, such as the construction and use of libraries' (Day, 1997). Suzanne Briet developed these ideas in her *Qu'est-ce que la documentation?* of 1951, in which she declared unequivocally: 'Un document est une preuve à l'appui d'un fait' and consequently archivists, librarians and museum curators were all engaged in the work of documentation (Briet, 1951, 9, 15 and 71; Maack, 2004, 738). Such an emphasis implies reference that permits knowledge to be 'organized within "dynamic", "rapid", and "precise" systems, grounded in standardization and documentary organization' (Day, 2001, 728).

In two pioneering papers Michael Buckland explored from this perspective the ontology of documents in the analogue and digital environments (Buckland, 1997 and 1998). In the second paper, 'What is a digital document', he argued: 'If we sustain the functional view of what constitutes a document, we should expect documents to take different forms in the contexts of different technologies and so we should expect the range of what could be considered a document to be different in digital and paper environments' (Section 6, page 228). With my colleagues, I have contributed to this debate, concluding in our most recent paper 'since it is content that is our fundamental concern, we must not concentrate on technology-driven solutions at the expense of the only thing about which questions of truth and validity are apt', and advise that we must 'learn from known practice and procedure in the analogue' (Allison et al., 2005; Currall et al., 2008).

Critical in our view to understanding what is happening in the information landscape is the avoidance of setting 'the technical and the semantic up in a binary opposition', which we regard as the 'greatest obstacle to resolving the debates within the digital environment' (Currall et al., 2008). One of the principal reasons for such polarity is that much research into the digital is predicated on the assumption that technology is 'new' and that there have been no previous information revolutions. Neither of these premises can be sustained. From the moment drawing and writing were invented several thousand years ago, technology has been the handmaid of information. This relationship has attracted the attention of philosophers since Aristotle, who rarely, if ever, privileged the technical over the intellectual. For Aristotle 'techné' embraced both the semantic and the technical that is echoed in the thinking of modern scholars, such as Heidegger and Foucault, and in the business models of search engine providers. The problem for the search engine providers, as Brabazon rightly points out, is 'confusing quality and quantity of information' (Brabazon, 2007a, 37). This is self-evident, particularly as much of the information accessible across the web, lacking the mediation familiar in the print culture, would once have been described as manuscripts or ephemera and found its way into the archive or special collection. Unquestionably such content does not lack value, but it requires different techniques in its use and more caution in establishing its trustworthiness.

The tokens of trust in the print culture are imprints, names, positions and reputations of authors, and appearance of the book itself, whereas in manuscripts the tokens are more subtle and some of the information may have to be inferred from the content and context. Some of this practice has transferred to the digital, but often there are financial barriers to access mediated information, whereas there are none for the rest. More worryingly, some misleading information, such as phishing scams, has embedded tokens copied from mediated sites, while others have been cut and pasted out of context. This razing of epistemic hierarchies, combined with an 'interminable "interpretation" of relativism', troubles many commentators, who react by looking back to the old certainties of a positivist universe where knowledge, held in libraries, was mediated in the print culture (Bloom and Higgins, 2006). Keen is convinced that the internet, where 'audience and author become one' is transforming our culture into a 'cacophony'. 'Truth . . . is being "flattened" as we create an on demand, personalized version that reflects our own individual myopia. One person's truth becomes as "true" as anyone else's' (Keen, 2007, 7, 11). Others, such as Brabazon and Breivik and Gee, call for a greater emphasis on inculcating 'information literacy' by librarians and enjoin us heroically to agree that 'learning resources programs that provide information literacy skills are essential to the development of the independent lifelong learner' (Brabazon, 2007a; Breivik and Gee, 2006, 56). There is a positivist tendency in such arguments that implies that authenticity and veracity are somehow objective when in reality they are dynamic and culturally specific – 'an object that might appear perfectly authentic from one perspective may be considered to lack sufficient tokens of authenticity in another, and may later from both viewpoints be considered invalid' (Currall et al., 2008).

However well intentioned, neither approach is practical, given societal expectations and the economic pressures on the curatorial professions, except at the margins. In their introduction to 'Problematising Global Knowledge and the new Encyclopaedia Project', Mike Featherstone and Couze Venn emphasize the need to address 'the production and circulation of knowledge in a way which opens up a more dialogical space of engagement with different globalizing knowledges and their modes of authorisation'. They embrace relativism with a postmodern passion, 'We are becoming increasingly aware of different accounts of global history and various alternative modernities' (Featherstone and Venn, 2006, 1–2). As Himmelfarb observes: 'If I were given to conspiratorial theories, I might speculate that Bill Gates, the chairman of Microsoft, is a secret agent of Jacques Derrida, the high priest of postmodernism. For the new technology is the perfect medium for the new ideology. Surfing through cyberspace is a truly postmodernist experience, a liberation from what the postmodernist calls "linear thinking" – a logical rational mode of reasoning' (Himmelfarb, 1999, 617). For Featherstone and Venn the foundation of scholarly endeavour remains the archive and the library, however defined; but an archive and library that is now global and is 'lived under the will to archive' (Featherstone and Venn, 2006, 12). For them:

> Digital media enables us to think beyond the book, or the working desktop covered with piles of opened books, journals and photocopies as our writing resource base, to the screen with its own virtual desktop, writing space or window and Internet connections. Or better, it points to our various modes of to-ing and fro-ing between the two modalities.
>
> (Featherstone and Venn, 2006, 11)

Over a decade ago Miksa perceptively reflected on the possibility of the 'private library' that is the desktop, which he characterized as 'a denial of the modern library's public space' and 'a return to the library era that preceded the modern library when a library generally represented the private space of an individual or of a small group'. Far from being nervous about such an outcome, he welcomed it and expanded Ranganathan's aphorisms 'Every reader his book', and 'Every book its reader' to read 'Every reader his library', and 'Every library its reader' – or as Nicholas would have us believe 'Every consumer his library' and 'Every library its consumer' (Miksa, 1996, 13; Ranganathan, 1931). Verne Harris (2001) from an archival perspective is convinced that attempts by the information professions to impose order on such private information space is a 'fool's errand' – 'instincts to tame, to destroy, or to flee promise impoverishment'.

Privileging public and private spaces

Such an approach works with the flow of societal expectations, but against library 'service orientated' provision and posits a return to the collection base as one of the resources that will stock the shelves of the private space. The library will indeed be a 'one-of-a-kind' archive that will privilege resources through subscriptions, links and through its holdings both physical and virtual. It may have 'internet cafes', but these may become as redundant as telephone kiosks. What it will have is reading rooms where the 'archive' can be consulted and where in the time-honoured tradition users can obtain advice to improve their search and 'literacy' skills. In much the same way that the binary opposition between the technical and semantic has been unhelpful, so too has that between 'free text searching' and the privileging of the catalogue and the search room. The two complement rather than work against each other as Lynch proposed (Lynch, 2003). As Miksa rightly pointed out 'a library is a sense-making and value-adding process applied to the bibliographic universe, an effort to bring some sort of useful control (i.e., bibliographic control) to a segment of the whole. At its core it constitutes a thoughtfully selected collection from among all possible informational objects placed in a rationally organized space for a designated target user population'. He dismissed as a mistake the notion that the undifferentiated contents of the internet could in any sense be thought of as a library, preferring to define it as 'an extension of the bibliographic universe, an extension that promises only to increase the size of the whole by orders of magnitude' (Miksa, 1996, 14). His vision implied convergence, but was in no sense monopolistic, and by placing emphasis on 'enabling' collection building in private space overlooked the process of selection, appraisal or privileging for preservation. We can see these ideas being played out on social networks that have adapted what appear to be bibliographic techniques in encouraging participants to tag their content to assist retrieval (Wesch, 2007).

Unless selection is to be defined anything more than heuristically as it is in most search engines, the 'privileging of the better and, by default, the non-privileging of the rest, remains a significant needed service' (Buckland, 1992). This is a value-laden statement that appears to contradict much contemporary thought, for example Nora's attack on *lieux de mémoire*, and implies that user demand will to some extent be directed or instrumented. As Currall, Stuart and I have argued, privileging is inevitable if information is to be more than an instantiation at a moment in time. If it is accepted that it is 'socially constructed, and not something objectively determined by a set of easily articulated criteria' as we do, the moral and political implications can be addressed. In achieving a plurality of provision that matches both Jeanneney's and Featherstone and Venn's expectations, we warn against 'monolithic control vocabularies' and urge greater openness, a dialogic process if you like, in setting selection criteria that agree with the conclusions of Nicholas and his colleagues in Chapter 6 (Currall et al., 2006).

The activities of selection and appraisal have become confused in discussion of digital curation with preservation for several, at times, conflicting reasons – there is reputedly more of it than ever before, there is the potential to keep everything, and lastly it is expensive to store and maintain (Harvey, 2005, 2007). The technical niceties of preservation are not of concern here and anyway as Ross has commented 'after more than twenty years of research in digital curation and preservation, the actual theories, methods and technologies that can either foster or ensure digital longevity remain startlingly limited' (Ross, 2006, 142). What is of concern is the imperative to preserve a selection of digital content in what we might call a 'digital repository' or library irrespective of complementary initiatives to capture the content of the web as a whole, such as Brewster Kahle's Internet archive, akin to Borges's nightmare Library of Babel (Borges, 1998). The starting point for any discussion must be the ontological status ('thatness' and 'whatness') of the objects. As we have seen, most digital objects that might be selected for preservation exist as single instantiations, even when they share characteristics with the mediated print culture, and consequently require a standard of care and conservation more often found in archives than in libraries. Since digital content that is mediated can easily be repurposed and repackaged and the cost of storage is relatively trivial, owners are less likely to release the 'original', suggesting that Winston's analysis that in the digital environment libraries 'may look more like museums where one-of-a-kind archives are held' may be correct (Beaudoin, 2006, 280).

The archival imperative

Where archives differ from libraries is that, at least in Western democracies, they have a juridical function protected by the rule of law to hold information fiduciarily that can be accessed by the public to call the executive to account and to allow history to be written (Moss, 2008). Although this function is analogous to the holding of canonical texts in the libraries of antiquity, it equates, as we have seen, more with Levy's notion of a 'shared sacred place', a receptacle of evidence as much as cultural artefact. Indeed Jenkinson, one of the leading archival thinkers in the United Kingdom, placed the 'sanctity of evidence' at the top of his archival creed (Jenkinson, 1980, 258). Without such a creed the archivist is powerless to defend the archive when governments seek to pervert it, as in Stalinist Russia, or deliberately do not tell the truth as would seem to be the case in the conduct of the war in Iraq by the United States (Chandrasekaran, 2006). The neo-conservatives have cynically manipulated postmodern thinking to assert 'truth is not salutary, but dangerous, and even destructive to society –

any society', and we could substitute archive for truth (Drury, 1997, 1). In other words if truth is unknowable, there is no need to tell the truth. This is made all the more easy in a digital environment where context is often absent and the processes involved in creating documents in the analogue built up over centuries have been abandoned, making it difficult to assert with any confidence that an object can be safely treated as evidence (Moss, 2005b). Keen cites the example of Al Gore's Penguin Army on YouTube that appears to be an amateur production but was in fact produced by DCI Group, a right-wing Washington public relations and lobbying firm (Keen, 2007, 13). This state of affairs is further complicated by our audit culture where as Strathern puts it the 'ought' becomes 'is' and things do indeed work backwards, where 'the form in which the outcome is to be described is known in advance' (Strathern, 2000). If this is the case then we would do well not to confuse accountability with memory or what Terry Cook calls puzzlingly, but admittedly from a different perspective, 'evidence and memory' (Cook, 2000). For these reasons we need, in appraising and selecting digital assets for preservation, to look to the disintermediated content of the web, as at least some, when taken together, combine to form 'social network architectures and collaborative models for cultural resistance' (Rhinehart, 2003). Blogs may well provide better insights into the war in Iraq or our contemporary culture than resources constrained either by deliberate deception, surveillance or audit. In his blanket attack on blogs Keen fails to consider that individual voices, such as that of Anne Frank or David Berger, both victims of the holocaust, have always contributed to the writing of history (Keen, 2007). As I have argued, the public archive in an open society protected by the rule of law must always have the potential to be subversive, to collect the soldier blogs that provide a different perspective on events in Iraq, or even to preserve records in defiance of executive instruction (Moss 2005a and 2006). The challenges for the information community are to develop the tools and techniques to select and capture this content, establish its provenance and then to make it available to the user community over a long period of time. With experience of privileging, appraisal and selection built up over centuries in the analogue, it is well placed to discharge this responsibility.

The repository from these perspectives to be 'trusted' must be mandated by a community, a city, a state, or an organization that defines and resources its purpose and collecting policies and offers protection through the rule of law, communal action or peer review to the contents. There is and will continue to be nothing to prevent digital content providers and social networks calling themselves archives, libraries or museums, but without a mandate they will lack credibility in the community of users they seek to serve and be as it were one-of-a-kind 'phishing archives'. One of the dangers of the retreat of the information professions into their curatorial gulags is that they become self-referential and lack justification and support. Stock selection becomes their preserve in direct contrast to much societal expectation, lacking the dialogic process essential in maintaining the satisfaction of both the sponsor and the customer. For the user building a private library, *caveat emptor* will always apply, even for content drawn from 'trusted repositories' and to this extent Brabazon and others are right to call for greater emphasis on information literacy in the classroom; but we need to remember that such literacy in the analogue is rarely generic but highly differentiated and itself often mediated by those with the appropriate skills and knowledge.

Those planning a holiday soon learn which sites to 'trust', biologists know which sites are suspect and government agencies know which sites to monitor. There are always barriers to entry that require users to grasp ontological and taxonomic knowledge before they can make effective use of an information resource. I cannot begin collecting Barbie dolls unless I know what they are and have some understanding of their individual characteristics. Rebalancing information services away from service delivery towards collection development might appear outmoded, but if search engines are allowed to drill down into holdings then they can be left to provide the distribution channel and consumer profiling, leaving curators to get on with what they are best at rather than trying foolishly to compete by writing their own algorithms. This after all is how the retail trade is taking advantage of the most powerful distribution channel the world has ever known; stock selection, categorization and presentation is arguably more important than customer service. The Queen then may find Buckingham

Palace library a more conducive place to read her book, uninterrupted by rows about prayer books, boundaries and marriages that would probably be negotiated in future on a social network.

References

Allison, A., Currall, J., Moss, M. and Stuart, S. (2005) Digital Identity Matters, *Journal of the American Society for Information Science and Technology*, **56** (4), 364–72.

Atkinson, R. (1990) Text Mutability and Collection Administration, *Library Acquisitions: Practice and Theory*, **14** (4), 355–8.

Beaudoin, M. (ed.) (2006) *Perspectives on Higher Education in the Digital Age*, Nova Science Publishers.

Bennett, A. (2007) *An Uncommon Reader*, Faber & Faber.

Berndtson, M. (2002) *Dreaming the Future. Some Funky Ideas on Managing Tomorrow's Library*, Bertelsmann Foundation.

Berndtson, M. (2006) *The Post Modern Library Space*, (Naples), www.naple.info/helsinki/maija_berndtson.pdf.

Bibliotheca Alexandrina (2008), www.bibalex.org/libraries/presentation/static/15110.aspx (February 2008).

Bloom, C. and Higgins, J. (2006) You, Sir, Are a Cad, a Cheat and a Bounder, *THES*, 15 September, 16–17.

Borges, J. L. (1998) *Fictions*, Penguin.

Brabazon, T. (2007a) *The University of Google – education in the post information age*, Ashgate Publishing.

Brabazon, T. (2007b) Boomers in Thrall to a Wiki Universe, *THES*, 6 November, www.timeshighereducation.co.uk/story.asp?sectioncode=26&storycode=311129.

Breivik, P. S. and Gee, E. G. (2006) *Higher Education in the Internet Age*, Praeger and the American Council on Education.

Briet, S. (1951) *Qu'est-ce que la documentation?* (Paris: EDIT), trans. Day, R. E., Martinet, L. and Anghelescu, H. (2006) *What is Documentation?*, Scarecrow Press.

Buckland, M. (1992) *What Will Collection Developers Do?*, *6 Supplement, Redesigning Library Services*, American Library Association, http://sunsite.berkeley.edu/Literature/Library/Redesigning/supplement.html.

Buckland, M. (1997) What is a Document?, *Journal of the American Society of Information Science*, **48** (9), 804–9.

Buckland, M. (1998) What is a Digital Document?, *Document Numérique* (Paris), **2** (2), 221–30.

Burke, P. (2000) *A Social History of Knowledge from Gutenberg to Diderot*, Polity.

Casson, L. (2001) *Libraries in the Ancient World*, Yale University Press.

Chandrasekaran, R. (2006) *Imperial Life in the Emerald City: Inside Iraq's Green Zone*, Knopf.

Clanchy, M. T. (1979) *From Memory to the Written Record*, Edward Arnold.

Coates, T. (2005) Our Public Libraries are in Dire Need of Renewal, *Society Guardian*, 7 September, www.guardian.co.uk/society/2005/sep/07/thinktanks.thinktanks.

Cook, T. (2000) *Beyond the Screen: the records continuum and archival cultural heritage*, paper delivered at the Australian Society of Archivists Conference, Melbourne, 18 August, www.mybestdocs.com/cookt-beyondthescreen-000818.htm.

Currall, J., Moss, M. and Stuart, S. (2006) Privileging Information is Inevitable, *Archives and Manuscripts – Journal of the Australian Society of Archivists*, **34**, 98–122.

Currall, J., Moss, M. and Stuart, S. (2008) Authenticity: a red herring?, *Journal of Applied Logic*, special issue on identity forthcoming.

Day, R. E. (1994) Diagrammatic Bodies. In Chia, C. H. (ed.) (1998), *Organized Worlds: explorations in technology and organization with Robert Cooper*, Routledge, 95–107, http://ella.slis.indiana.edu/%7Eroday/cooper.htm.

Day, R. E. (1996) LIS, Method, and Postmodern Science, *Journal of Education for Library and Information Science*, **37** (4), 317–24, http://ella.slis.indiana.edu/%7Eroday/method.html.

Day, R. E. (1997) Paul Otlet's Book and the Writing of Social Space, *Journal of the American Society for Information Science*, **48** (4), 310–17.

Day, R. E. (2001) Totality and Representation: a history of knowledge management through European documentation, critical modernity, and post-Fordism, *Journal of the American Society for Information Science and Technology*, **52** (9), 725–35.

Dempsey, L. (2000) Scientific, Industrial, and Cultural Heritage: a shared approach

– a research framework for digital libraries, museums and archives, *Ariadne*, 22, www.ariadne.ac.uk/issue22/dempsey/.

Derrida, J. (1996) *Archive Fever: a Freudian impression*, University of Chicago Press.

Drury, S. B. (1997) *Leo Strauss and the American Right*, Palgrave Macmillan, http://rightweb.irc-online.org/analysis/2004/0402nsai.php.

Featherstone, M. and Venn, C. (2006) Problematising Global Knowledge and the New Encyclopaedia Project, *Theory, Culture & Society*, **23** (2–3), 1–20.

Foucault, M. (1990) *The History of Sexuality*, Vol. 1, *An Introduction*, trans. Hurley, R., Vintage.

Glosiene, A. and Manzhukh, Z. (2005) Towards a Usability Framework for Memory Institutions, *New Library World*, **106** (7/8), 303–19.

Greenfield, S. (2006) We Are at Risk of Losing our Imagination, *The Guardian*, 25 April, http://education.guardian.co.uk/schools/comment/story/0,,1760235,00.html.

Harris, V. (2001) On the Back of a Tiger: deconstructive possibilities in 'Evidence of Me', *Archives and Manuscripts*, **24** (1), 8–23, www.mybestdocs.com/harris-v-tiger-edited0105.htm.

Harvey, R. (2005) *Preserving Digital Materials*, K. G. Saur.

Harvey, R. (2007) *Instalment on 'Appraisal and Selection'*, DCC/Digital Curation Manual (Glasgow: DCC), www.dcc.ac.uk/resource/curation-manual/chapters/appraisal-and-selection/.

Heidegger, M. (1962) *Being and Time*, trans. Macquarrie, J. and Robinson, E., SCM Press.

Heidegger, M. (1978) *Basic Writings*, Krell, D.F. (ed.), Routledge.

Himmelfarb, G. (1999) Revolution in the Library, *Library Trends*, **47** (4), 612–19.

Jeanneney, J. (2006) *Google and the Myth of Universal Knowledge*, The University of Chicago Press.

Jenkinson, H. (1980) *Selected Writings of Sir Hilary Jenkinson*, Ellis, R. and Walne, P. (eds), Alan Sutton.

JISC (2006) *Designing Spaces for Effective Learning*, www.jiscinfonet.ac.uk/infokits/learning-space-design/dsel.

Keen, A. (2007) *The Cult of the Amateur – How Today's Internet is Killing Our Culture and Assaulting Our Economy*, Doubleday.

Lanier, J. (2006) Digital Maoism: the hazards of the new online collectivism, *Edge:*

the Third Culture, www.edge.org/3rd_culture/lanier06/lanier06_index.html.

Levy, D. M. (2001) *Scrolling Forward – Making Sense of Documents in the Digital Age,* Arcade Publishing.

Lucas, C. (1985) Introduction. In Le Goff, J. and Nora, P. (eds), *Constructing the Past – essays in historical methodology,* Cambridge University Press.

Lynch, C. A. (2003) Colliding with the Real World: heresies and unexplored questions about audience, economics, and control of digital libraries. In Bishop, A., Butterfield, B. and Van House, N. (eds), *Digital Library Use: social practice in design and evaluation,* The MIT Press, 191–218.

Maack, M. N. (2004) The Lady and the Antelope: Suzanne Briet's contribution to the French documentation movement, *Library Trends,* **52** (4), 719–47.

Malpas, J. (2005) Hans-Georg Gadamer, *Stanford Encyclopaedia of Philosophy,* http://plato.stanford.edu/entries/gadamer/#3 (January 2008).

Mathieson, S. A. (2004) Libraries Embrace Digital Age, *The Guardian,* (28 January), www.guardian.co.uk/society/2004/jan/28/epublic.technology12.

Miksa, F. L. and Doty, P. (1994) *Intellectual Realities and the Digital Library,* University of Texas, www.csdl.tamu.edu/DL94/paper/miksa.html.

Miksa, F. L. (1996) The Cultural Legacy of the 'Modern Library' for the Future, *Journal of Education for Library and Information Science,* **37** (2), 100–19.

Moss, M. (2005a) Archivist: friend or foe? *Records Management Journal,* **15** (2), 104–14, also in Aubry, M., Chave, I. and Doom, V. (eds) (2007), *Archives, archivistes et archivistique dans l'Europe du Nord-Ouest de l'Antiquité à nos jours : Entre gouvernance et mémoire,* Institut de Recherches Historiques du Septentrion, Université Charles-de-Gaulle, Lille, 243–53.

Moss, M. (2005b) The Hutton Inquiry, the President of Nigeria and What the Butler Hoped to See?, *English Historical Review,* **CXX** (487), 577–92.

Moss, M. (2006) The Function of the Archive. In Moss, M. and Tough, A. (eds), *Record Keeping in a Hybrid Environment – Managing the creation, use and disposal of unpublished information objects in context,* Chandos Press, 227–43.

Moss, M. (2008) Opening Pandora's Box – What is an archive in the digital environment?. In Craven, L. (ed.), *What are Archives?,* Ashgate.

Nora, P. (1996–8) *Realms of Memory: Rethinking the French Past,* 3 vols, Columbia University Press.

Ormiston, G. and Schrift, A. (eds) (1990) *The Hermeneutic Tradition,* SUNY Press.

Otlet, P. (1934) *Traité de documentation: le livre sur le livre: théorie et pratique*, Editiones Mundaneum, Palais Mondial.

Ranganathan, S. R. (1931) *Five Laws of Library Science*, Madras Library Association.

Ray, K. L. (2001) *The Postmodern Library in an Age of Assessment*, ACRL Tenth National Conference, www.ala.org/ala/acrl/acrlevents/kray.pdf.

Rhinehart, R. (2003) *A System of Formal Notation for Scoring Works of Digital and Variable Media Works of Art*, www.bampfa.berkeley.edu/about_bampfa/formalnotation.pdf.

Ross, S. (2006) Approaching Digital Preservation Holistically. In Moss, M. and Tough, A. (eds), *Record Keeping in a Hybrid Environment – Managing the creation, use and disposal of unpublished information objects in context*, Chandos Press, 115–53.

Schuermeyer, W. (1935) Aufgaben und Methoden der Dokumentation, *Zentralblatt für Bibliothekswesen*, **52**, 533–43. Reprinted in Frank, P. R. (1978), *Von der Systematischen Bibliographie zur Dokumentation* (Wege der Forchung 144), Wissenschaftliche Buchgesellschaft).

Stille, A. (2002) *The Future of the Past*, Picador.

Strathern, M. (2000) *Abstraction and Decontextualisation: an anthropological comment or: e for ethnography*, http://virtualsociety.sbs.ox.ac.uk/GRpapers/strathern.htm.

Surowiecki, J. (2004) *The Wisdom of Crowds: why the many are smarter than the few and how collective wisdom shapes business, economies, societies and nations*, Doubleday.

Wesch, M. (2007) *Information Revolution*, www.youtube.com/watch?v=-4CV05HyAbM.

Wisner, W. (2000) *Whither the Postmodern Library?: libraries, technology, and education*, McFarland.

Wolf, F. A. and Buttman, Ph. (1807) *Museum der Altertumswissenschaft*, Reimer.

Wood, H. H. and Byatt, A. S. (2008) *Memory and Anthology*, Chatto & Windus.

5

The psychology of the digital information consumer

BARRIE GUNTER

Summary

Online or computer-mediated communication (CMC) has witnessed widespread penetration into many areas of life – personal and professional. Divorced from the physical or non-verbal cues that characterize face-to-face (FtF) communication, where the communication of emotion can be as significant as the communication of information, how do we cope? Research has indicated that in CMC settings, we compensate for the loss of FtF cues by filling the gaps and expanding upon what limited information we may receive about another person online to construct an impression of that person. In addition, when dealing with automated CMC systems we may find ourselves reacting to computer technology as we would another person. We like it if it is nice to us and dislike it if it is not. Understanding the rules of online interpersonal and human–computer interaction can provide important insights into how to utilize more effectively, and how to design more user-friendly, online communications systems.

Introduction

Internet penetration has displayed dramatic growth in a spell spanning little over a decade with almost one in five people in the world now online. In 1995, fewer than half of 1% of people in the world (16 million) used the internet. By 2000, this figure had grown to 451 million (7%+ of world population) and crashed through the one billion user mark by 2005 (1,018 million; 16% of world population). By the final quarter of 2007, internet penetration had reached 1.2 billion users (www.internetworldstats, 2007). In some parts of the world, internet penetration levels are even more impressive with most people in the USA (70%), over half of those in Australia/Oceania (55%) and approaching half in Europe (42%) being online. It is not just the scale of the online world that is remarkable but also the way it has transformed the lives of people who use it. For the new community of digital information consumers around the world, the internet and its associated online technology have opened huge repositories of content and access to services that cater to almost every need.

The internet has become established as a major source of information and entertainment for many people and also the site of an increasingly diverse array of transactions. It is fast emerging as the world's premier communications medium, being used for a wide range of personal, professional and business, and public communications on a one-to-one, one-to-many and many-to-many basis.

In terms of general internet activities, a number of studies conducted in the USA, Europe and within the UK have indicated that the internet is used for a range of information, entertainment and interpersonal communication purposes. Information uses include general interests such as news, sports, weather and other more personalized information connected to health, finances, travel, education and hobbies (Hitlin and Rainie, 2005; Madden, 2005; Ofcom, 2007a). Entertainment uses include live consumption of online audio and video content, and downloading of such content (Rainie, Kalechoff and Hess, 2002; Ofcom, 2007b). Transactional uses cover a wide range of business, professional and social activities (Dutton and Helsper, 2007).

Research in the USA reported by the Pew Internet and American Life Project showed that by 2005 clear majorities of internet users across all age-bands went online to use e-mail (91%), get health information (79%), conduct product research (78%), get news (73%), conduct online purchases (67%), and make travel reservations (63%). Overwhelming majorities of teenagers in particular also went online to play online games (81%), do school research (81%), and send/receive instant messages (75%). One in two 29 to 39-year-olds bank online (50%). Nearly two-thirds of 40 to 49-year-olds (64%) used government websites (Madden, 2005).

By the end of 2002, virtually all UK internet users (99%) sent and received e-mail, an overwhelming proportion got their news information online (89%) and significant proportions went online for work purposes (69%), to look for information linked to a hobby or interest (65%), and to find product-related information (62%). Internet users already made online purchases, with the great proportion having bought books or made travel reservations online (80% in each case) and over half using the internet to buy groceries (51%) (Gunter et al., 2003).

The same survey found that over seven in ten internet users (71%) had conducted personal banking online in the previous year and nearly half (49%) had done so in the previous week. Most online users said they had, in the previous week, contacted a friend (88%) or relative (60%) via e-mail which in each case exceeded the proportions saying they had telephoned or visited friends and relatives.

The social dimension of the internet has always represented an important part of its applications repertoire and has become a rapidly growing phenomenon in the middle of the first decade of the 21st century. The use of online social networking sites has exhibited dramatic growth especially among young people aged 16 to 24 years (iProspect, 2007). Nearly one quarter of European internet users (23%) indicated in 2006 that they visited social networking websites at least once a month, a figure that reached as high as one in three internet users aged 16 to 24 years (European Interactive Advertising Association, 2007). Later research about internet use in the UK in 2007 by the Oxford Internet Institute reported that interactive online communications remained among the primary online applications. Many of these applications had a social dimension. The emergence of more advanced and sophisticated uses of the internet for content creation and social networking purposes, while growing in popularity, were largely from minorities of internet users (Dutton and Helsper, 2007). Nearly all UK internet users said they checked e-mail (93%) and many (60%) also said they engaged in instant messaging. Far fewer engaged with chat rooms (29%) or blogging (12%).

In the US, while only a minority of the general population (16%) said in 2005 that they used online social networking sites, this figure grew dramatically to over half (55%) of 12 to 17-year-olds (Lenhart, 2007; Lenhart, Madden and Hitlin, 2005). While more people across age groups report using the internet for a variety of purposes, the younger internet users – the digital consumers of the future – have displayed a clear tendency to adopt more complex interactive applications more quickly with the informational and social dimensions of online activities often becoming conflated.

Understanding personal digital consumption

Although the world wide web represents a huge repository of information on just about any subject we can think of, the internet has achieved significance for its ability to provide information of personal importance to us. One of the biggest information-related uses of the internet of this kind is the search for health advice. Most internet users have been found to go online to obtain health information (Nicholas et al., 2003). In the UK, 80% of internet users said they access health content online, while smaller proportions had engaged in other health-related activities such as participated in an online support group (14%), e-mailed their doctor (10%) or sought online advice from a doctor (8%).

Given the growing significance of online sources for important communication transactions, it is essential that we understand how people engage, psychologically, with these technologies. This principle is critical in contexts where people go online and seek advice or information that could have great significance for their lives or even in other settings where financial costs are involved. It is also important that online service providers are aware of difficulties digital consumers experience when interacting with online systems and services that fail to deliver what they seek, or do so only with great effort on the part of consumers themselves.

One important question to ask is whether online communication always works effectively. In the health context again, most online health information seekers in the United States (74%) indicated that they were reassured by the information they found on some occasions, but others indicated sometimes to being overwhelmed (25%), frustrated (22%), confused (18%), or even frightened (10%) by what they found (Fox, 2006).

One reason why it is important to study the psychology of the digital information consumer is also to understand why some people remain offline. The reasons people give for not using the internet in the UK are that it is 'too difficult' (64% agreed with this sentiment in 2007 compared with 56% in 2005). Many users (49%), and more especially non-users (79%), of the internet simply remark that it is 'too complex'. Others – both users (29%) and non-users (56%) – said that it was 'frustrating to work with' (Dutton and Helsper, 2007).

Thus, people can become confused online. There may be critical communication issues that undermine effective use of the internet. This could seriously affect the successful completion of online transactions or the ability to establish effective interpersonal relations. We therefore need to understand how people engage with online communications. This means examining the rules of communication and the orientations people can adopt towards information technologies. A critical and fundamental question is: 'How good is the internet as a communications medium?' Is online communication always effective? The answer, it seems, depends upon the application. It is vitally important to know how to ensure that online communication works effectively because of the growing range of consumer, business and professional transactions that take place over the internet.

Media richness and mediated communication

Information can be communicated in a number of different formats and channels in the online world. Information can be held and transmitted as text, audio sequences, images or a combination of these modes. In judging the effectiveness of information transmission the benchmark that is normally invoked is face-to-face communication. Face-to-face is regarded as the richest form of communication because information can be conveyed in verbal and non-verbal forms (Rice, 1993). It is also possible effectively to communicate emotion as well as factual content. Other forms of communication, such as text and audio, remove some of the critical ingredients – especially non-verbal ones – rendering communication less 'rich'.

Within the online environment, the absence of non-verbal cues that play such an important part in face-to-face communication can encourage people to behave differently – often in a more uninhibited fashion. This is because computer-mediated communication bestows a degree of anonymity on those communicating with each other and reduces the influence of social factors that would determine appropriate ways to behave in offline communications settings in which people confront one another face to face (Kiesler and Sproull, 1992; Siegel et al., 1986).

In an online setting, therefore, communicative interactions that are text-based – including e-mail, instant messaging, and live online social networks – create a sense of anonymity and personal identity dilution. This set of circumstances can undermine effective communication and transferral of information. In a digital consumer context this situation could be critical if a breakdown in communication results in transaction failure or damage to the reputation of an online service provider. All is not lost, however. Evidence has emerged that shows that we often try to overcome the limitations of online text-based communication by seeking out information about those whom we cannot see or hear online in order to create as positive an impression about them as we can (Walther, 1992; 1997). Sometimes, this impression formation process can take longer than it would in face-to-face communication settings (Walther, 1992; Walther and Burgoon, 1992). Sometimes, stereotyped or false impressions can materialize (Spears and Lea, 1992; Walther, 1997). Nonetheless, skilled use of subtle linguistic and non-linguistic (symbolic) devices in this environment can enhance communication effectiveness even though we can neither see nor hear the people we are interacting with (Walther and Tidwell, 1995; Walther and D'Addario, 2001). Using such paralinguistic devices, significant and fruitful online relationships can be established (Walther, 1992). In fact, hyperpersonal relationships can sometimes emerge via online links that can be every bit as close as ones developed through face-to-face interactions (Walther, 1997; Walther, Slovacek and Tidwell, 2001).

In the absence of non-verbal cues that we take for granted in normal face-to-face interactions, in a computer-mediated communication setting we may be driven to adopt different interpersonal strategies when interacting with other people. One finding has been that we may be less likely when meeting strangers online to engage in 'small talk' than we would if we met them in person. We may also be more likely to ask them more direct questions about themselves touching, more quickly than we would in a face-to-face meeting, on intimate disclosures. If both participants readily engage in this type of behaviour, strong 'hyperpersonal' bonds can become established more quickly than they would in a face-to-face setting (Tidwell and Walther, 2002).

The term 'social presence' has been coined to express the degree to which mediated communications channels create a sense of the presence of others such as would be automatically characteristic of face-to-face communication settings (Short, Williams and Christie, 1976; Williams and Rice, 1983). Face-to-face communication offers the greatest 'social presence' of any form of communication. A rich form of communication is characterized by having the ability to convey information with a minimum of ambiguity, to provide an immediate feedback loop between those engaged in communicating, to create a feeling of immediacy, to provide a more personalized form of communication, and, of course, to communicate emotion (Trevino, Lengel and Daft, 1987).

The degree of social presence afforded by mediated communications, such as online or computer-mediated communication, depends upon the communications format adopted. Video- or audio-conferencing can enable communicators to see and/or hear each other. Hence, cues associated with posture, physical gestures or movements and facial expression together with voice tone, volume and other personal characteristics linked to vocal expressions may be available. In a text format, however, these cues are all missing.

Studies of 'media richness' rankings of different communication modes have been produced. In one study, the highest rating for media richness was assigned to face-to-face communication, followed by telephone communication, desktop video, voice mail, written text (hard copy) and finally e-mail (Rice, 1993). Given that there are perceived differences in the quality of communication afforded by these different communications modalities, are there also different or similar rules of engagement that apply to communications interactions as well? While communicating via text, which is the most common form of online communication, but is not as 'rich' or does not offer the same degree of 'social presence' as face-to-face interaction, do the same rules of effective communication apply in each case?

There is a growing body of empirical evidence on the subject of computer-mediated communication that has provided valuable insights into the way we communicate online, especially when we interact with other people whom we cannot see or hear. This work has fuelled several important theories that begin to provide explanations of how to achieve effective communication online. One significant observation is that in computer-mediated communications systems in which text-based communicating dominates (or is the only one available) we lose our sense of identity (Postmes and Spears, 1997). Such communications systems, in a sense, hide who we are, and create a sense of anonymity. This loss of identity has been examined conceptually by de-individuation theory that has indicated that under these conditions the usual social norms and constraints that govern communication behaviour may be weakened (Postmes and Spears, 1997). Such conditions can sometimes encourage more impulsive and less controlled behaviour and the use of rude or even inflammatory language (Lea et al., 1992).

Although the anonymity of online communication can create conditions in which people may communicate with each other in a less than constructive fashion, other evidence has emerged that even though the standard norms of social conduct can become diluted in mediated communications systems, when we use these systems we nevertheless seek ways of maximizing the success of remote social or professional relationships. We do this by trying to glean as much information as we can about the people with whom we are communicating, even though we cannot see or hear them. According to social information processing theory (SIPT) we strive to maximize positive meaningful relations when communicating with others online (Tanis and Postmes, 2003).

In following up on this point, one finding is that when we communicate with others online via text, we tend to assign crude characteristics to these unseen others on the basis of the social groups to which we believe they belong. Social identity de-individuation (SIDE) theory has been developed to provide an explanation of this process (Postmes and Spears, 1997). What this means, however, is that when people communicate online they behave in accordance with prejudices about the types of others they believe they are in communication with. In fact, the de-individuation process can magnify the degree to which we seek to establish the identity of others online, using any scraps of information we may be able to obtain about them. What this may mean in practice is that we construct generalizations about individuals about whom we may have only superficial information. This can lead to exaggerated attributions based on generic information, usually linked to the social group(s) or demographic category to which we establish they belong. Thus computer-mediated communication can enhance the significance of group membership from which we invoke group-level expectations about another, otherwise anonymous, individual with whom we are communicating online (Spears and Lea, 1992).

We need to break this theory down before considering empirical evidence that supports it. De-individuation refers to a psychological state involving decreased identity or self-awareness. This state can occur readily in online communications settings in which communicators cannot see or hear one another. In face-to-face transactions, we form impressions of other people on the basis of what they say, but also on the basis of how they say what they say as well as how they appear. In other words, both verbal and non-verbal information is used to form judgements about others. When communicating via text, there are no non-verbal cues available to us about the other person. Under such circumstances, therefore, online communicators use superficial social cues to assign characteristics to others online on the basis of the social groups to which they are believed to belong. Such generalizations can result in people formulating inaccurate perceptions of shared similarities or dissimilarities with others with whom they are communicating online. Such generalizations can, in turn, determine the impressions we form about unseen or unheard others online which in turn influence the opinions we develop about them as people in specific behavioural contexts, including determination of their perceived status, authority or competence in relation to specific activities (Postmes, Spears and Lea, 2000).

Some examples of de-individuated behaviour

In a test of SIDE and SIPT, one study had participants evaluate online discussion partners. The participants entered into online discussions on selected topics and then subsequently rated their discussion partners on a number of evaluative scales. The evaluative ratings indicated whether participants had a clear or ambiguous impression of their discussion partner. Other ratings indicated how positive participants felt about their discussion partners (Tanis and Postmes, 2003). In some conditions, participants were also presented with a picture of their discussion partner or a brief written biography about them. Seeing a picture or reading a biography reduced the ambiguity of feelings about the discussion partner. Seeing a picture also made participants feel more positive about their discussion partner. Results indicated that more personalized information about someone online can alter impressions of this other person to make them more certain and more favourable.

In a further experiment, participants were told that discussion partners were either from their university (in-group) or from a different university (out-group). In some cases, social cues such as a picture or biography of a discussion partner were present and in others they were absent. SIDE would predict that in the absence of social cues, we identify more closely with people we believe to be like ourselves. This hypothesis was supported in the current study because in the absence of social cues, in-group members were preferred over out-group members. When pictures or biographies were provided, however, in-group versus out-group differences were much diluted (Tanis and Postmes, 2003).

These findings showed that provision of additional personalized social cues about online discussion partners added to the overall richness of the communication. There was more likelihood that social prejudices would distort impressions when minimal social cues were provided about another person with whom communication took place in a text format. When personalized information was provided about other discussion partners online, these social category stereotypes and prejudices disappeared. It is important to know about these psychological dynamics in relation to online communication. The presence of social cues may be highly significant in communication contexts in which people need to co-operate with each other, particularly where social prejudices might operate against the achievement of group cohesion.

Another important aspect of online communication is the way computer interfaces visually represent other people on screen. Such electronic representations have been found to influence how we respond to other people with whom we are communicating remotely when we cannot see or hear them. One investigation of this subject invited college students to take part in experiments in which they engaged in an exercise that involved reaching high-risk versus low-risk decisions about the actions of others in fictional scenarios (Lee and Nass, 2002). In one experiment, participants were randomly allocated to conditions in which they believed they were taking part in judgemental tasks with real people online and in a second experiment, participants were similarly allocated, but told that their judgements were being made alongside the decisions of computers. In each case, online judgements were made in the presence of either one other person or computer, or four other people or computers.

To begin with participants were presented with verbal descriptions of fictional scenarios in which an individual was faced with a decision about a course of action to take – for instance, in relation to an educational or a job/career choice in which the options being made available carried either a low risk or high risk in terms of possible outcomes. A series of decision choice options was provided to the participants in each case. Before they made their own recommendations, they saw the recommendations of the other human or computer judges. In some conditions, also, participants were told that their recommendations would be shown to the other judges (i.e. made public) or that this would not happen (i.e. recommendations kept private).

The participants' judgments were examined for conformity or non-conformity with recommendations of other participants. Previous psychological research had indicated that there is a stronger tendency to conform with group decisions if the remainder of that group reach a consensus viewpoint on an issue (Asch, 1958). One question was whether the same social–psychological dynamics would apply in the online world.

Another key manipulated variable in this experiment was the way the responses of 'other' participants were represented on screen. There were three conditions. In one condition, the other participants' recommendations were shown as text in 'textboxes'. In a second condition, the recommendations were shown in text bubbles with stick men. In the third condition, the recommendations were shown in text bubbles with animated cartoon-like characters. While the stick men and textboxes all looked alike, the animated cartoon characters were distinctive.

Results from the first study in which participants believed they were interacting with other people online showed that participants' agreement with 'other' remote participants' recommendations was more likely to occur when there were four 'others' (all in agreement) than when there was just one 'other'. This was true whether participants' opinions were made publicly and openly or privately and not shown to others. The group effect, however, was not as strong when participants made their views known in private. Further, while participants in general were more inclined to disagree with others online when there was only one other person making judgements with them, this tendency was stronger when judgements were made privately than publicly (Lee and Nass, 2002).

There was also an effect of on-screen iconic representation of other participants on agreement with their opinions, but this effect occurred mostly in respect of judgements made publicly and much less so with judgements made privately. There was greater public compliance with others' recommendations when these 'others' were represented simply as textboxes on screen than as either animated cartoon characters or stick men. Other participants were perceived as more competent, trustworthy and attractive, however, when represented as cartoon figures than in the other visual formats.

The stronger group conformity effect in conditions in which other people online were visually represented in exactly the same way (e.g. textboxes) rather than when represented as distinctive characters (cartoon representations) was explained by the on-screen sameness of others reinforcing the sense that they were a 'group'. This effect is explained by SIDE theory. Textboxes all looked alike and did not differentiate between other participants. This meant that they were more likely to be treated as a single group with a common identity. Cartoon characters individualized other participants while not disclosing their real identity and this diluted the group cohesion effect. There was no satisfactory explanation offered of why there were differences in evaluative perceptions of other participants linked to on-screen representation. It is possible, however, that participants did make judgements based on appearance of on-screen characters. Cartoon-like screen characters were anthropomorphized and treated more like they were real people (Lee and Nass, 2002).

In a second experiment, the same researchers (Lee and Nass, 2002) used a similar design but instructed participants that they would interact with computer agents rather than other people online. In other words, the decision-point recommendations were made by intelligent technologies rather than by other people. The researchers wanted to find out here whether similar social dynamics would occur in relation to participants' recommendations and tendency to exhibit group conformity behaviour.

Results showed no indication of group conformity effects whether participants made their own recommendations publicly or privately. Participants were no more likely to agree with a consensus view of four computers than the view of a single computer. Hence while group conformity effects can occur in computer-mediated communication interactions with other people, when judgements were made publicly, they did not occur in human–computer interaction settings.

The visual representation of computer agents on screen, however, did exert an effect on the publicly and privately voiced recommendations of participants. Once again, as with online interactions with other human participants, group conformity was strongest in human–computer interactions when the computer agents were shown on screen as textboxes. In terms of evaluative perceptions, an interesting set of differences occurred between perceptions of human online participants and computer agents online whereby although both were regarded as equally competent and trustworthy, human interactants bestowed a stronger feeling of social presence than did computer agents (Lee and Nass, 2002).

This research offers insights into the way people behave towards others online and into the social dynamics that occur in the online world. In many ways, the norms of social engagement known to occur in the offline world also occur in the online world. These social dynamics occur when we communicate online with other people whom we cannot see or hear. Sometimes these dynamics can affect the way we respond when we know we are communicating with machines rather than humans online, though the potency of these dynamics may be somewhat diluted in the latter case. In the next part of this chapter, further research is reported that underlines still further how technologies can be anthropomorphized in human–computer interactions.

Treating technology as people

It is apparent from research with computer-mediated communication that psychological principles from the offline world also apply in the online world. Taking this principle one step further, there are times when we treat the technology with which we are interacting in the online world as if it is another person. This phenomenon has been described in terms of 'the media equation' where media technology and the world with which we engage is treated the same way as real life (Reeves and Nass, 1996). Put simply, people have been found to treat computers in the same way that they treat other people and respond to computers as they respond to other people. Understanding these principles and how they operate in practice can have important implications for software and interface design.

Reeves and Nass (1996) reported a series of experiments that were designed to demonstrate 'the media equation'. In one study which they titled 'the polite computer' they set up conditions in their laboratory in which student participants played a game with a computer. The computer had 20 questions to ask of the participant to guess the name of a type of animal. For example, the computer could ask 'Does the animal have four legs?' or 'Is the animal a reptile?' and so on. The participant could suggest better questions to improve the computer's chance of guessing correctly. Usually the computer guessed wrong.

There were three conditions in this experiment. In one condition, the game was played through to completion and then followed by another game. In a second condition, at the end of each game the computer reacted to the help received from the participant in a positive way, saying how helpful the participant's question suggestion had been. In the third condition, at the end of each game the computer reacted negatively saying how unhelpful the participant's question suggestions had been.

In rating themselves afterwards, participants who had been flattered by the computer thought they had done a significantly better job at picking questions compared with those in the other conditions. Participants who had been flattered by the computer also said they liked it more as compared with those in the other two conditions. In other words, human participants responded to a technological device in a similar fashion to the way they would have been expected to react to another person who had flattered or criticized them.

In a further study, Reeves and Nass (1996) examined how participants reacted to a computer that was critical not just of their performance but also of the performance of another computer. Participants were initially tutored by a computer with an audio speaker that presented information with voice as well as text. After the tutoring session the participants were evaluated on their learning by moving to a second computer with a different voice. As well as having their answers marked as correct or incorrect, the assessing computer offered either positive or negative comments about the tutoring ability of the first computer. Some participants then returned to the first computer where it self-evaluated its own performance either positively or negatively. Other participants moved to a third computer with yet a different voice that again offered praise or criticism of the first computer's tutoring performance.

In general, participants thought the first computer did better when it was praised than when it was criticized. When the tutoring session was praised this also caused participants to believe that their own performance had been better than it really was. They disliked computers that were critical of other computers, but they liked a computer more if it was self-critical. Reeves and Nass noted that these findings model the way we evaluate other people. We tend to dislike overly critical people and we tend to like people who are modest and self-effacing. The same social principles seem to apply when we assess machines with human characteristics.

How important are these findings?

The internet has become a site of diverse searches and transactions for significant and growing numbers of people. It provides access to huge volumes of information and has also emerged as a primary communications medium through which we can maintain social contacts and conduct our personal and professional business. Online communications can be conducted with other people and with automated transactional systems. Much of the communication conducted online, however, takes place in text formats. This means that much online communication lacks the richness of direct communication conducted face to face. As such, a great deal of valuable information that we would normally use to judge other people is not available to us in the online environment. In this setting it is important to understand whether the same rules of social and interpersonal engagement apply as those that govern our behaviour in the offline world. Hence, understanding how to utilize online or computer-mediated communications effectively and knowing how people respond to automated, yet slightly humanized, online systems is vitally important in an era where so much of what we do in our every-day lives involves this form of communication. We need to know how people engage with each other through online technology and we also need to know how they engage with technology itself.

Limited social cues about other people with whom we are communicating online can result in distorted perceptions about them. These perceptions are very real and can underline impressions formed about others online and sometimes undermine effectively relationship formation or transactions. Introducing just a few personalized social cues about another person online can produce a radical shift in responses to that person and influence the way we behave towards them. In effect, when communicating with other people online, certain established norms of social interaction in the offline world are applied in the online world. The absence of the same richness of information about another person, when we can neither see nor hear them online, may encourage us to take short-cuts in impression formation. With the small amount of information we have about them we may construct stereotyped identities of them that may not reflect their true identities. When this happens, our evaluations of the other person online may be prejudicial and inaccurate.

Technology itself can become anthropomorphized – that is, it can take on human qualities. On some occasions this can happen even though we interact with technology via text-based communication. If further humanizing characteristics are added, such as a human voice (or even an artificial, human-like voice), the treatment of technology as 'human' can become even more pronounced. The principles underpinning the way we respond to humanized technology would seem to derive from general social principles and codes of practice developed in the offline world. Knowing how these principles work in the online world can be helpful in understanding how people interact with technology and can provide useful input to interface design.

References

Asch, S. E. (1958) Effects of Group Pressure upon the Modification and Distortion of Judgments. In Maccoby, E. E., Newcomb, T. M. and Hartley, E. L. (eds), *Readings in Social Psychology*, Rinehart and Winston, Inc.

Dutton, W. and Helsper, E. J. (2007) *The Internet in Britain – 2007*, Oxford Internet Institute, www.oii.ox.ac.uk/microsites/oxis.

European Interactive Advertising Association (2007) *Social Networking to Drive Next Wave of Internet Usage*, www.eiaa.net/news/eiaa-articles-details.asp?id=1068.

Fox, S. (2006) *Are 'Wired Seniors' Sitting Ducks? Data Memo*, Pew Internet and American Life Project, Washington DC, (April), www.pewinternet.org.

Gunter, B., Russell, C., Withey, R. and Nicholas, D. (2003) The British Life and Internet Project: inaugural survey findings, *Aslib Proceedings*, **44** (4), 203–16.

Hitlin, P. and Rainie, L, (2005) *Teens, Technology and School. Data Memo*, Pew Internet and American Life Project, Washington DC, (August), www.pewinternet.org.

iProspect (2007) *Social Networking User Behaviour Study*, (April), www.iprospect.com/about/researchstudy_2007_socialnetworkingbehavior.

Kiesler, S. and Sproull, L. (1992) Group Decision Making and Communication Technology, *Organizational Behaviour and Human Decision Processes*, **52**, 96–123.

Lea, M., O'Shea, T., Fung, P. and Spears, R. (1992) 'Flaming' in Computer-Mediated Communication: observations, explanations, implications. In Lea, M. (ed.), *Contexts of Computer-Mediated Communication*, Harvester Wheatsheaf, 89–112.

Lee, E. J. and Nass, C. (2002) Experimental Test of Normative Group Influence and Representation Effects in Computer-Mediated Communication. When interacting via computers differs from interacting with computers, *Human Communication Research*, **28** (3), 349–81.

Lenhart, A. (2007) *Social Networking Websites and Teens: an overview*, Pew Internet and American Life Project, Washington DC, (January), www.pewinternet.org.

Lenhart, A., Madden, M. and Hitlin, P. (2005) *Teens and Technology*, Pew Internet and American Life Project, Washington DC, (July), www.pewinternet.org.

Madden, M. (2005) *Generations Online*, Pew Internet and American Life Project, Washington DC, (December), www.pewinternet.org.

Nicholas, D., Huntington, P., Gunter, B., Russell, C. and Withey, R. (2003) The British and their Use of the Web for Health Information and Advice: a survey, *Aslib Proceedings*, **55** (5+6), 261–76.

Ofcom (2007a) *Public Service Broadcasting Annual Report*, (March), Office for Communications, www.ofcom.org.uk.

Ofcom (2007b) *The Future of Children's Television Programming: Research Report*, (October), Office for Communications, www.ofcom.org.uk.

Postmes, T. and Spears, R. (1997) *Quality of Decisions, Group Norms and Social Identity: biased sampling or sampled biases*, Paper presented at the Fifth Munster Workshop on the Social Identity Approach, Rothenberge, Germany.

Postmes, T., Spears, R. and Lea, M. (2000) The Formation of Group Norms in Computer-Mediated Communication, *Human Communication Research*, **26**, 341–71.

Rainie, L., Kalechoff, M. and Hess, D. (2002) *College Students and the Web*, Pew Internet and American Life Project, Washington DC, (September), www.pewinternet.org.

Reeves, B. and Nass, C. (1996) *The Media Equation: how people treat computers, television and new media like real people and places*, Cambridge University Press.

Rice, R. E. (1993) Media Appropriateness: using social presence theory to compare traditional and new organisational media, *Human Communication Research*, **19** (4), 415–84.

Short, J., Williams, E. and Christie, B. (1976) *The Social Psychology of Telecommunications*, Wiley.

Siegel, J., Dubrovsky, S., Kiesler, T. and McGuire, T. N. (1986) Group Processes in Computer-Mediated Communication, *Organizational Behaviour and Human Decision Processes*, **37**, 157–87.

Spears, R. and Lea, M. (1992) Social Influence and the Influence of the 'Social' in Computer-Mediated Communication. In Lea, M. (ed.), *Context of Computer-Mediated Communication*, Harvester Wheatsheaf, 31–65.

Tanis, M. and Postmes, T. (2003) Social Cues and Impression Formation in CMC, *Journal of Communication*, **53** (4), 676–93.

Tidwell, L. C. and Walther, J. B. (2002) Computer-Mediated Communication Effects on Disclosure, Impressions, and Interpersonal Evaluations: getting to know one another a bit at a time, *Human Communication Research*, **28** (3), 317–48.

Trevino, L. K., Lengel, R. H. and Daft, R. L. (1987) Media Symbolism, Media Richness and Media Choice in Organisations: a symbolic interactionist perspective, *Human Communication Research*, **14** (3), 553–75.

Walther, J. B. (1992) Interpersonal Effects in Computer-Mediated Interaction: a relational perspective, *Communication Research*, **19** (1), 52–90.

Walther, J. B. (1997) Group and Interpersonal Effects in International Computer-Mediated Collaboration, *Human Communication Research*, **23** (3), 342–69.

Walther, J. B., and Burgoon, J. K. (1992) Relational Communication in Computer-Mediated Interaction, *Communication Research*, **19**, 50–88.

Walther, J. B. and D'Addario, K. P. (2001) The Impacts of Emotions on Message Interpretation in Computer-Mediated Communication, *Social Science Computer Review*, **19**, 323–45.

Walther, J. B., Slovacek, C. and Tidwell, L. C. (2001) Is a Picture Worth a Thousand Words? Photographic images in long term and short term virtual teams, *Human Communication Research*, **28**, 105–34.

Walther, J. B. and Tidwell, L. C. (1995) Nonverbal Clues in Computer-Mediated Communication and the Effects of Chronemics on Relational Communication, *Journal of Organizational Computing*, **5**, 355–78.

Williams, F. and Rice, R. E. (1983) Communication Research and the New Media Technologies. In Rostrom, R. N. (ed.), *Communication Yearbook* 7, Sage, 200–4.

6

The information-seeking behaviour of the digital consumer: case study – the virtual scholar

DAVID NICHOLAS
PAUL HUNTINGTON
HAMID R. JAMALI
TOM DOBROWOLSKI

Summary

This is a lynchpin chapter in that preceding chapters have provided the essential context for it and the following ones feed off it, and its relative significance is reflected by the greater space devoted to it. The massive exodus of the information user from the physical space to the virtual space and the opening up of information resources to millions of people who once had poor access to information resources requires us all to reflect on what this really means in information-seeking terms. This chapter enables this reflection by profiling and evaluating the information-seeking behaviour of the digital information consumer. This is largely undertaken by visiting the huge evidence base that the CIBER research group have amassed over the years during the Virtual Scholar research programme (2001–8), the biggest of its kind ever conducted. The evidence base is formed from the millions of digital footprints that people leave behind them after a visit to a digital resource. Using deep log analysis techniques, sense has been made of these data and they are stitched together to create information-seeking portraits for a wide range of scholarly communities, including staff, students and researchers. Via these portraits, user satisfaction and scholarly outcomes are investigated.

It has to be said that the characteristics of the information-seeking behaviour once uncovered come as something of a revelation, and are very different to what might have been expected from reading the established literature on information seeking. The behaviour resembles more that of an e-shopper confronted by the cornucopia of shopping opportunities offered by the web. It is frenetic, promiscuous, volatile and viewing in nature, and, as such, requires us all to radically rethink information provision and delivery to the digital information consumer.

Background

The internet has moved into all corners of our life, online searching has become a daily activity for millions and millions of people. A fundamental shift in the information domain has occurred: science and the public sector are no longer the biggest markets for online services. In recognition of this CIBER (www.ucl.ac.uk/slais/research/ciber/) has spent the past seven years evaluating the information-seeking behaviour of a number of emergent, strategic digital information communities, most notably those associated with news (Nicholas et al., 2000), health (Nicholas, Huntington, Jamali and Williams, 2007), voluntary and charitable work (Nicholas, Williams and Dennis, 2004) and scholarly publishing. Despite the fact that these communities are clearly very different in make-up they have all been shown to demonstrate a very similar and highly distinctive form of information seeking, something that is due to the fact that they are all using a common platform, the internet, for domestic, leisure and work purposes. This form of information seeking has more in common with the behaviour of shoppers than with that of traditional library users. This is because there is now a huge, rich market for information and obtaining information is part of the shopping experience. As shoppers it is our duty to be smart shoppers who play the market. Nobody wants to spend too much time and money and obtain the wrong things.

That is why we prefer the term digital information 'consumers' rather than 'users' to remind ourselves of this; and we believe that it is the very failure to recognize this which is causing the current professional angst over the future of the information professions.

In this chapter we will describe and evaluate this consumer form of information seeking by making reference to a vast evidence bank generated by CIBER's most recent research programme, covering the information-seeking behaviour of hundreds of thousands of virtual scholars. We shall also look at the implications of this form of behaviour for information providers of all types, libraries, publishers and academe. It is a very, very different form of behaviour than what one might have expected to find from reading the classic information-seeking texts of Ellis and Haugan (1997) and Wilson (1999). This is partly because we have undergone a massive paradigm shift in information-seeking behaviour since they developed their ideas and partly because it has only recently been possible to observe information-seeking behaviour on a huge scale and in minute detail. The digital consumer revolution requires us to consign a good deal of what we know about the information-seeking behaviour of the virtual scholar to the bin.

The methodology and evidence base

The evidence that informs our portrayal of the information-seeking behaviour of the virtual scholar largely comes from the digital footprints (logs) that millions of scholars left behind them when they visited some of the world's most important scholarly databases like ScienceDirect (www.sciencedirect.com), OhioLINK (www.ohiolink.edu), Synergy (www.blackwell-synergy.com), Oxford Open Journals (www.oxfordjournals.org/oxfordopen/), Oxford Scholarship Online (www.oxfordscholarship.com), Wiley Interscience (www.interscience.wiley.com), Intute (www.intute.ac.uk), and British Library Learning (www.bl.uk/learning/). These footprints have been collected and evaluated using a procedure called 'deep log analysis' which converts the data in the transactional logs held on the servers into meaningful information-seeking characteristics for scholarly communities and then enables that data to be related to academic satisfaction and outcomes. There are three types of data – activity or use data (Table 6.1), information-seeking characteristics (Table 6.2 on page 118) and user data (Table 6.3 on page 120), and 27 individual data points that can be extracted – an enormous yield. In addition logs provide indicators of satisfaction; where this is the case it is mentioned in the tables.

Table 6.1 Key features of the digital information footprint of the virtual scholar: activity or use data

Activity metric	Explanation and significance	Notes
Number of pages viewed	This is an aggregated, disassembled figure, that provides estimates on the raw volume of use. It needs to be borne in mind that much of what is demanded is not wanted and hence we need additional measures of use to obtain the complete picture.	Activity measures provide the dimensions and weight of the user footprint.
		These 10 activity metrics give us a 360 degree view of use. They enable us to categorize and distinguish users by their short/long, frequent/infrequent and heavy/light usage.
		Enables comparisons to be made between 'persistent' or core and 'bouncing' or light users.
		A number of metrics point to levels of **satisfaction** or genuine use and together provide strong overall indicators of consumption.
Number of full-text downloads	This is the usage gold standard metric; it is said to provide valuable information on user interest or **satisfaction**. But it is also 'suspect' and needs triangulation with the other activity metrics listed in this table. People sometimes do not read what they download or view.	
Number of sessions conducted	Sessions, or 'visits', provide *the* vehicle for the investigation of information-seeking behaviour because they bring together related information events.	

Continued on next page

Table 6.1 *Continued*

Site penetration	The number of views per session, a possible 'busyness', interest and **satisfaction** metric.	
Time spent viewing a page	Another aggregate figure, which helps distinguish between casual/unsatisfied use and more substantial use and greater interest. A possible **satisfaction** metric.	
Time spent on a session	Together with site penetration, identifies the more substantial or deeper user sessions. Provides a measure of **satisfaction** and, importantly, evidence of reading online.	
Number of searches undertaken in a session	Demonstrates the level of interaction and is also another 'busyness' metric. It could also point to problems in finding what is wanted – repeated searching showing frustration in finding what is wanted. This is also a searching metric, see below.	
Number of repeat visits made	A powerful metric indicating need, loyalty and **satisfaction**. A high number of visits is an indicator of a core or persistent user. The number of visits made can be partly explained by the extent of the current awareness need and turnover of data on the site. This metric is difficult to measure because of the difficulties in identifying the returnee, because of floating IP addresses and proxy servers.	
Number of journals used	This is an aggregate figure, which says something about the level of take-up, the reach/range of activity and relevance of the service.	
Number of views per journal	Provides those popular ranked tables of journal use and a guide to the extent of scatter/concentration of use.	

Table 6.2 Key features of the digital information footprint of the virtual scholar: information-seeking characteristics

	Information-seeking characteristic	Explanation and significance	Notes (Most of these analyses are conducted within the session metric)
Type of content viewed	Number of journals used in a session	This is an indicator of interdisciplinarity, interest, and scatter. It also tells us something about the type of information need – current awareness, fact-finding etc. It can help to identify persistent users.	Describes the key characteristics of the footprint, its complexity and sophistication.
	Names of journals used	This helps determine whether the journals are highly ISI ranked or not, so show something about the 'level' and quality of use.	
	Subject of journal used	This is the key interdisciplinarity indicator. It is also a surrogate for the user's subject background if this is not possible to obtain by other means.	
	Age of journal used	A currency indicator, which is, possibly, also a characteristic of a persistent user. There are problems of determining the exact dates because sometimes the online version comes out earlier than the date published on the print issue. So it is sometimes best to use categories – current, recent and old etc.	
Type of material viewed	Type of full-text view	HTML v PDF. The latter is probably a very good indicator of **satisfaction**, especially if the article is viewed first in HTML and then PDF.	For instance, home page, abstracts, table of contents, full-text, search/browse facilities. People use abstracts to power browse and preference for abstract over the full text can indicate short attention spans and the unwillingness to read online. As mentioned earlier, the full-text view is thought to be especially important, as it is the gold standard metric, the one librarians use to determine whether they are getting value for money for their subscription.

Continued on next page

Table 6.2 *Continued*			
	Size of article used	Long/short articles, measured by page numbers. Says something about the propensity to read on- and off-line and the length of attention spans.	
	Publication status of article	The logs of ScienceDirect provide the opportunity to evaluate the publication status of an article, whether it was an article in press or the finally published article. A possible indicator of the need for current information.	
Searching style	Search approach adopted	Whether using menus, search engines, or both. Tells us something about the predilection for browsing or searching, whether someone knows what they are looking for or not.	Points to possible information needs traits – current awareness, fact-finding and also to the depth and complexity of searching.
	Number of searches conducted in a session	Says something about the level of engagement.	
	Number of search terms used in search	Provides evidence of the type of search, complexity of the search and/or the sophistication of the searcher.	
	Form of navigation	The referrer link used (or place from where the user came), for instance search engine, library link, PubMed or similar.	

Thus deep log analysis provides a dataset unparalleled in terms of detail. It provides a record of everything that someone does online, while they are viewing, searching, browsing and navigating over the period surveyed (for instance, 15 months as was the case in the OhioLINK study). The methodology has other major advantages:

1 Logs record the use of everyone who happens to engage with the system and therefore the data yield and reach are absolutely enormous. There is no need to take a sample and thus the tricky question of representativeness does not even arise, although, of course, by definition non–users are not covered.

Table 6.3 Key features of the digital information footprint of the virtual scholar: user characteristics

User characteristic	Explanation and significance	Notes
Subject/discipline	Obtained from the subject of journal, the sub-network label of the computer used (where this is meaningful and stable), and subscriber data, where this is available.	By combining activity and information-seeking metrics (searching and type of content viewed) with user characteristics we can identify diversity in take-up, and, possibly, best practice, which, of course, will require explanation through survey and qualitative methods.
Academic status	Derived from the sub-network label. For instance, used to identify places from where students and academics might be more likely to use the system. Can also be obtained from a subscriber database, if linked to the log entry.	
Geographical location	Obtainable from the IP address and DNS look-up.	
Institution	Obtainable from the IP address.	
Type of organization used to access the service	Detected via the IP address and it is possible to determine whether it is an ISP, academic institution etc. Academic institution identification is much more accurate and robust.	
User demographics	If subscriber data can be captured from logs then it is possible to obtain information on age, gender and academic status.	

2   Logs provide a direct and immediately available record of what people have done: not what they say they might, or would, do; not what they were prompted to say, not what they thought they did. Logs do not rely on memory they provide 'honest' data.

3   The data are collected routinely, automatically and quite anonymously. There is no need to contact the user or obtain their co-operation as the 'users' under investigation are computers, not individuals.

Every methodology comes with its problems too and it would only be right to present these here:

1   Weblogs provide a user 'trace' – a computer, but not real user or individual identification. Typically all there is to work on is the Internet Protocol (IP) number, which provides the name of the institution and country to which the user belongs. It is only by means of deep log analysis that we can add demographic data to the trace.

2   Logs provide a partial picture of user activity. A user may well view a number of sites in collecting data to meet an information need. With logs you are usually looking at just one site option.

3   Robots account for a good deal of usage. Thousands of robots or agents harvest information on the world wide web for a wide variety of purposes – indexing, caching and data mining, for instance. Robots inflate usage statistics by as much as 50%. Deep log analysis methods enable a far more accurate identification of robot use.

Use counts are not completely accurate

Caching: this impacts on page view counts as some viewed pages are not recorded or attributed to a user's search session, leading to more sessions being classified as having viewed fewer pages. Caching is the storing of previously viewed pages on to the client's computer; repeat in-session accesses to these pages are made from the cache and are not requested from the website's server and hence not recorded in the logs, something that underestimates use.

Proxy connections: a proxy connection is one where a number of computers are connected to the internet via a single IP number. In such cases, session details of the connected computers are muddled together and it appears that all use comes from the same 'proxy' user since users are identified by IP numbers. This leads to an underestimation of the number of users and sessions.

Session definition: the way sessions are defined can lead to variations in counting. Sessions are, sometimes, identified in the logs by an identification number. In such cases logs include a session-beginning tag and a session-ending tag, which enables us to make time calculations as well. Unfortunately, as far as the logs are concerned, nobody logs off on the web: they just depart anonymously. Typically, then, to estimate a log-off – or a session end, and so define a session – a time lapse of inactivity has to be assumed and the industry standard tends to be 30 minutes but CIBER uses a much more accurate (lower) estimation based on page viewing times, which is more like 8–12 minutes.

Estimating time spent online: page view time is estimated by calculating the difference in time between one page and the next page viewed. No estimate can be generated for the last page viewed in a session because, as previously mentioned, there is no log-off recorded in the logs.

Double counting: if someone views a full-text document in HTML format and then goes on to view this item in PDF, proprietary software tends to count this as two views. This particularly arises where the user comes in from a gateway or third-party site and that site only indexes the HTML version. Hence, when the user clicks through to the article, the user is served up with the HTML version. To view the PDF version the user has to come out of the HTML full-text version and load up the PDF format version. This process results in the downloading of two items rather than one and can considerably inflate the gold standard full-text metric. CIBER analyses allow for this by only counting this as one download if the PDF view follows shortly after the HTML view.

These data provide us with a firm foundation for forecasting the behaviour of the future virtual scholar and a reality check against which to judge the veracity of the floods of user research generated by the ubiquitous questionnaire and focus group.

Information seeking

The scholarly world, like the news, health and shopping worlds, has experienced an earthquake that has registered at the top end of the Richter scale and we are still experiencing the aftershocks, and will do for some years to come. The earthquake being referred to is the one triggered by the internet which has led to the mass migration of scholarly information-seeking to the virtual space, a process which is gaining considerable momentum as a result of the two latest aftershocks – e-books and social networking sites. After each aftershock new users are brought into the scholarly net and changes occur in the information-seeking behaviour of the population at large. But we are talking here about evolutionary, incremental and not revolutionary change. The fundamental 'consumer' characteristics of the information consumer, as those of the e-shopper, have already been laid down and are now becoming widely known through the work of CIBER (Naughton, 2008).

As mentioned earlier, thanks to the digital transition a large and increasing amount of the information-seeking behaviour of scholars has become visible and can be monitored comprehensively, remotely and in real-time. A sea change has occurred and this should command attention, not just because of what it tells us about the world of the virtual scholar but also because it provides information about aspects of information-seeking behaviour that have not previously been observable, and about which people have often had to guess.

Scholarly information seeking today, like consumer information-seeking generally, has been shaped by a number of factors, most notably: disinter-mediation (which means, no mediation, serve yourself to information), easy access to the product, the provision of massive choice, reliance on search engine searching and a much wider range of people being brought into the scholarly net, e-shoppers, for instance. This has created a consumer market for scholarly information products and a very distinctive 'consumer' form of behaviour, one that Chris Russell has described in Chapter 3. For most people who are presented with the realities of this form of behaviour, it comes as something of a revelation, and, for some, it is very disturbing too. In broad terms this behaviour can be portrayed as being active (frenetic), horizontal, bouncing, navigating/checking and viewing in nature. It is also promiscuous, diverse and volatile. Surprisingly, too, it is not just centred on the viewing of full-text documents, supposedly the diamonds in the scholarly mine, much navigating is undertaken too. The journey through cyberspace is either inter-esting in itself (because of the fascinating things you can find) or it is confus-ing, and people are having to trek all over the place to find what they want. The truth is probably both are true. Much of it is also robotic (see page 140).

It is pretty obvious that this form of behaviour presents serious challenges to traditional information providers, nurtured in a hard-copy paradigm and, in many respects, still tied to it. No one surely would have described scholarly information-seeking behaviour in these terms, rather it was thought to be staid, conservative and loyal; far from it.

In the coming pages we shall examine 13 key aspects of digital information-seeking behaviour: activity, volatility, horizontal, navigating, viewing, diversity, checking, access expectation, robotic, internationality, currency, interdisciplinarity and scatter. Following the information-seeking analysis there is an examination of the impacts on (and obstacles to) information seeking (featuring Web 2.0 and open access publishing) and then a consideration of the outcomes of information seeking.

1 Activity

Standard methods of calculating use, like so-called 'hit' or page counts, tend to exaggerate site activity because they include robot use, count duplicate views (e.g. where a PDF and HTML view of a document counts as two downloads) and use which is clearly not positive (the viewing of irrelevant pages served up in spades by a search engine). Nevertheless, even using the much more robust measures employed by CIBER log analysis (see Table 6.1), the levels of activity associated with a scholarly site, as in the case of retail sites, are very impressive indeed and seem to be rising inexorably. Undoubtedly, scholarly information sites are exceptionally popular. Two things make them popular and are powering their growth: the existence of a huge mass of non-subscribers coming in via search engines, people who do not have full access rights, but who are interested in the product and who by their sheer numbers dwarf the site's core audience; the fact that the core audience can access the site any time and anywhere thanks to broadband, wireless, the Blackberry, mobile phone and the like. Not only are more people being drawn into the scholarly net, but existing users can search much more freely and flexibly than ever before, so racking up their use. Apart from time, there appear to be few obstacles to information seeking. The (pleasant) shock for many people is how big the appeal is for the product, which is surely a huge relief to the information professions, when there is so much else to worry them.

A potted selection of CIBER e-journal usage statistics illustrates the point extremely well. As far back as 2003 the Blackwell Synergy database (www.blackwell-synergy.com) attracted more than 500,000 people to its site a month, and these people made five million views during their visits; more recently (2005–6) on the OhioLINK service 2,250,000 pages were viewed and 339,000 sessions conducted in 15 months. In the case of OhioLINK (www.ohiolink.edu), an e-journal platform, which provides access to the full text of some 6000 journals, in a single month in 2007 all bar five of the journals were used, so disproving the notion that much material available is not being used and that authors are only publishing for themselves (or their mothers!). Two-thirds of visitors to Emerald (www.emeraldinsight.com), an e-journal site covering business and information management journals, turned out to be non-subscribers, people who did not have full-text rights and were simply happy with an abstract or whatever full text was being offered free at the time. In the case of *Nucleic Acids Research* (nar.oxfordjournals.org), a highly specialist journal, really only accessible to experienced researchers in the field, usage increased by 150% in three years as a direct result of opening the site to search engines (Nicholas, Huntington and Jamali, 2007). Intute, a scholarly gateway site that acts as a validated signpost to scholarly websites (www.intute.ac.uk) saw six million pages viewed in a matter of just three months in 2007.

How does all this activity square with the concerns that dominated the profession 20 years ago that the huge availability of data would result in overload? Well, in interviews we have conducted with academics in 2008, the term rarely ever came up and when the interviewer prompted the interviewees, they simply shrugged their shoulders. They are resigned to it; it is just part of the scenery or the academic assault course, and it is a small price to pay for the unbelievable level of access obtained. It is almost as if they do not want to rock the boat because that would sink it. They remember the 'bad' times.

The results of CIBER's SuperBook study (Nicholas, Huntington, Rowlands et al., 2007) showed that e-books will surely be the next scholarly publication success story, although if anything, demand could be even more spectacular than that we have seen with e-journals. After all, e-books have a much wider and larger audience many of whom – students and arts and humanities academics – have not fully benefited from the e-journal revolution. Students will lead the charge when they find that the supply of textbooks has finally been unblocked.

It is indeed ironic that it should be during a period of long and sustained growth in the provision and usage of scholarly publications that many librarians feel challenged and sidelined. The challenge for libraries arises from the fact that, as the scholar flees the physical space for the virtual space (and, as a result, becomes more energized), they move closer to the publisher and further from the library. As a direct consequence they become more anonymous and removed from the scene of scholarly information consumption, and librarians become correspondingly less informed about the behaviour of their users. So it is quite possible that librarians will be the only stakeholder group that will not benefit from a rapidly rising market for the scholarly product. Whether this will indeed be the case is being investigated by the authors on the JISC-funded UK National E-Books Observatory project (www.publishing.ucl.ac.uk/observatory.html). Such worries probably explain library moves to take the fight to publishers by establishing institutional and subject repositories.

Of course, the danger with high usage figures is that it engenders a high level of well-being and complacency; if there is so much demand for the service, why should we bother to change it or even investigate whether people are indeed happy or satisfied with the service?

2 Volatility

Not only is there a lot of growth associated with scholarly information services, there is also a good degree of volatility associated with them. Use varies enormously from year to year, term to term, month to month, by day of the week and hour of the day. Table 6.4 shows the year-to-year usage figures for the Emerald database for the period August 2001–January 2002 and August 2002–January 2003 for 91 universities. There is a huge see-sawing in use with

Table 6.4 Volatility in Emerald database use expressed as a percentage for 91 UK universities (2001–2 to 2002–3)

Movement	% Change
Increase	
More than 100%	11
+ 75–99%	2
+ 50–74%	3
+ 25–49%	16
+ 1–24%	29
Decrease	
– 1–24%	24
– 25–49%	10
– 50–74%	3
– 75–99%	1
Average	17

the majority of increases/decreases of the magnitude of 25% and over. In fact, 11% of universities increased their usage by more than 100%.

Although use is volatile it is often highly patterned. Thus use tends to peak in the autumn and spring terms and this is illustrated by Figure 6.1 (overleaf) which shows long-term usage patterns for the journal *Nucleic Acids Research*. Figure 6.1 also demonstrates the strong growth associated with most scholarly sites mentioned earlier. The dotted line denotes the date when the journal went open access, triggering further growth. Use is also generally strong during the week, tends to be highest on a Monday (as in the case of e-shoppers) and drops significantly over the weekend, with most use occurring between about 11am and 4pm during the day. This is shown in Figure 6.2 (see page 129) in regard to the usage of Oxford Scholarship Online, an e-monograph platform.

Patterns of usage also vary with e-platform, with e-textbooks usage more likely to be tied to the rhythms of the course/modules being studied.

It is the high levels of volatility that frighten off publishers from going down the road of introducing business models based purely on usage figures, they prefer the relative comfort zones created by 'big deals' and consortia

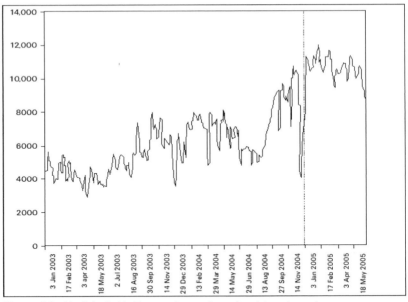

Figure 6.1 *Nucleic Acids Research*: number of articles viewed
January 2003–June 2005

agreements. A big deal is any online aggregation of e-content that a publisher, aggregator, or vendor offers for sale or lease at prices and/or terms that substantially encourage acquisition of the entire corpus (Peters, 2001).

3 Horizontal

Arguably, the most important CIBER finding has been the discovery of a widespread, pronounced and endemic form of digital information-seeking behaviour amongst scholars, best described as 'bouncing' although the description 'flicking' would do equally. Bouncing is a form of behaviour where users view only one or two web pages from the vast numbers available to them and a substantial proportion (usually the same ones) generally do not return to the same website very often, if at all. The actual figures regarding bouncing are well worth reflecting upon.

All the CIBER studies showed that around 55–65% of e-journal users typically view no more than three pages in a visit and then leave. The studies

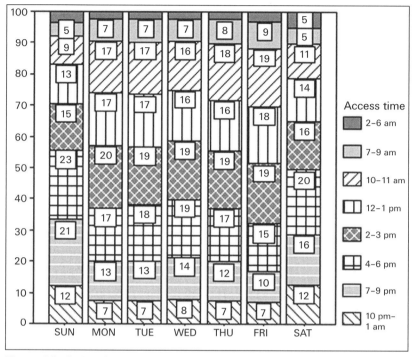

Figure 6.2 Oxford Scholarship Online – percentage distribution of access times (UK users only) across day of week

also showed around half of all users did not return or only returned after a prolonged gap.

Thus, in the case of the two most recent CIBER scholarly database evaluations, that of BL Learning and Intute which were conducted as part of the Google Generation project (CIBER, 2008), the figures for people viewing just one page and leaving were almost identical, respectively 57% and 58%. With regard to return visits, ScienceDirect data is illustrative (www.sciencedirect.com). Over a five-month period (January–May 2005) 40% just visited once, 24% visited 2–5 times, 15% visited 6–15 and 21% visited over 15 times.

This suggests, at best, a checking–comparing, dipping sort of behaviour that is a result of being provided with huge digital choice, search engines constantly refreshing that choice, and a shortage of time that results from so much to look at. In this respect the behaviour is best seen as being akin to television channel-hopping using the remote control – you flick around alighting on things of interest and when the interest fails or wanes you flick to something else. At worst, it points to possible failures at the terminal as a result of poor information literacy skills (significantly, the evidence also shows that young people are more inclined to bounce), lazy search engine searching, and poor content and poorly designed websites. The findings below (see page 134) regarding online viewing lend some weight to the 'failure' explanation.

In addition to younger people, search engine users and non-subscribers (often the same people) are more likely to bounce.

The significance of this for libraries and publishers is threefold:

1   They need to make their offerings suitable for bouncing by making their contents digitally visible and easily consumable by opening up their contents to search engines, enticing them in via abstracts, keywords, and other devices that feed the bouncing form of behaviour.
2   They should abandon any notion of being a one-stop shop, this is a fantasy in a world chock-full with choice.
3   They should accept the fact that much content will be seldom or never used, other than, maybe, as a place from which to bounce (a stop on the way). With increasing content choice and myriad routes to finding content (via social network sites, for instance) one might expect the bouncing rate to increase.

4 Navigating

Bouncing of course is partly a function of navigating your way towards content (and relevance), via a rich array of search and browse pathways, in a vast and constantly changing virtual space. It has been shown time and time again in CIBER studies of e-scholarly platforms, whatever the specific audience, that the majority of users (the proportion normally varies between about two-thirds and three-quarters) find the site through the use of Google and other search engines. This is very significant in a number of ways, as we shall go on to point out. Probably of most significance, though, is the fact that the user generally does not come in via the homepage (like the e-shopper), but drops

Table 6.5 Intute – search expressions used by search engine users to enter the site

Search expressions	Page	Directory
search?hl=en&safe=vss&q=How+do+we+ separate+gases+in+air&btnG=Search	p01014	sciences
search?q=wembley+twin++towers&hl=en &lr=&safe=vss&start=10&sa	fullrecord	social sciences
search?q=BBC.+CO.+%2FSCHOOLS+%2F KS3BITESIZE&btnG=Search	fullrecord	sciences
search?q=perfume+bottle+producers&hl= en&lr=&cr=countryUK|c	nwfa (glass)	artsandhumanities
search?hl=en&q=aerodynamics+in+cyclin g&meta=cr%3DcountryUK	fullrecord	sciences
search?hl=en&q=definitions+of+cleavage +lustre+etc&btnG=Search	search	sciences
search?q=+science+antique+items+for+sa le&hl=en&lr=&start=20&	search	sciences
search?hl=en&lr=&q=Chicago+world+war +ll+recruit+ad+posters&btnG=Search"	search	artsandhumanities
search?q=interactive+latin+dictionary&hl= en&lr=&safe=off&start=20&sa=N"	browse (200408)	artsandhumanities
search?hl=en&q=full+text+electrical+hvac +plumbing+book+manual+guide+online+f ree+&btnG=Google+Search"	search	sciences
search?q=librarian+costume&hl=en&lr=&s tart=60&sa=N"/	browse (artifact1047)	artsandhumanities

deep down into the site, as a selection of search expressions used in the case of the Intute service (www.intute.ac.uk) show (Table 6.5). This means that users probably short circuit completely the homepage that site owners have spent so much time and love on.

Do not be misled by Table 6.5, however, in fact today's scholars do not construct searches with many terms in them or conduct many searches in a session. Typically one-third of users enter one word in their search statements, about the same proportion two words and the remaining third three words or more. Just under half of all users employ just a single search during a session or visit and just over a quarter undertake two. With regard to searches, ScienceDirect data showed that in sessions where a search was undertaken, half saw just one search conducted, 35% saw 2–4 searches being conducted, 9% 5–10 and 1% over 10 searches.

Once into the site, scholars begin to engage with the myriad search and browse facilities provided. This can be seen in Figure 6.3 (overleaf), which shows the types of pages viewed by users of the e-monograph package

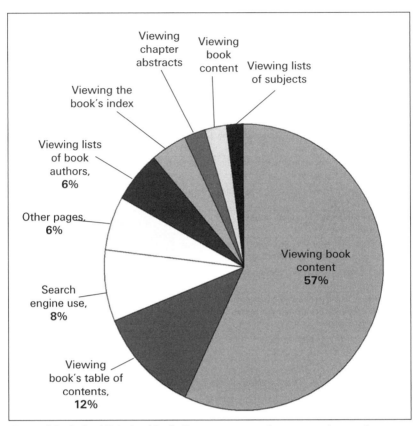

Viewing chapter abstracts

Viewing book content

Viewing lists of subjects

Viewing the book's index

Viewing lists of book authors, 6%

Other pages, 6%

Search engine use, 8%

Viewing book's table of contents, 12%

Viewing book content 57%

Figure 6.3 Oxford Scholarship Online: percentage frequency of type of page viewed

Oxford Scholarship Online (OSO), where just over half of all page views were to actual book (content) pages. All the other page views concerned browsing lists, inspecting contents pages, employing keywords, using search engines and examining abstracts for clues to content. There are many, many routes to finding content on OSO; they do not fall neatly into the browsing/search camps so favoured by librarians, and clearly users take advantage of the full range of these facilities.

An investigation of online use at four universities connected to the OhioLINK journals database provides further proof of the extent of navigating in a virtual environment. In this study, page views were classified into five groups, views to: menus, which included views to the alphabetical and subject menus of database (journal) content; lists, which included journal and issue lists; the search facility; abstracts; and full-text articles. Lists recorded, by some margin, the most views (719,674); they were followed by articles (580,164), the search option (364,713) and abstracts (258,772), with menu items accounting for 176,018 views. The general result supports the earlier statement that users undertake a wide range of actions online and viewing full-text articles was just one of them and not the most frequent one at that. Browsing and navigating towards text was clearly a significant form of behaviour in the case of large digital libraries like OhioLINK. Also, with more than a quarter of a million abstracts viewed, this has to be a powerful testament of the enduring popularity of abstracts – perfect, perhaps, for making choices in a crowded digital information environment, and this is especially significant in the case of OhioLINK where users did not have to view an abstract before they could view the full text, which is typically the case in other digital journal libraries.

The form of navigation adopted, perhaps not surprisingly, leads to very different usage patterns and outcomes. Thus by using internal and external search engines, users are provided with a much wider and disparate view of what is on offer and they are therefore forced to engage with a wider range of material – more titles, older material, from more subjects. This in turn leads inevitably to higher bouncing rates because much of the material served up by this form of wide-angled (shotgun) searching will inevitably be irrelevant.

As mentioned previously, younger people are more likely to use engines and this is partly explained by the fact that search engines, unlike browsing mechanisms like content, subject and alphabetic lists, do not require you to have any prior knowledge of the formal literature, its structure and hierarchy. This might well mean that future users will bring with them less knowledge of the scholarly system, of which libraries are currently an important component. If you reflect on the fact that most libraries were originally – and still are – designed so their contents could be browsed first, this is quite a fundamental shift and not yet reflected in information provision.

Interestingly, librarians have picked up on the popularity (and problems) of search engine searching and are developing their own engines to stop user flight. The latest initiative, and maybe the last hurrah, is federated retrieval, search software that searches across all their resources (catalogues, digital journal deals/collections and multimedia resources, possibly also learning material). It is believed that this will offer a trusted and effective searching environment missing from the big search engines and Google Scholar. With federated searching, librarians are bravely taking Google and the Google Generation head-on, believing retrieval is home ground for them. The early signs are quite promising.

5 Viewing

Bouncing can be construed to point to negative scholarly outcomes (not finding what you want, short attention spans, etc.), as does another piece of evidence, that concerning online viewing – on average most people spend only a few minutes on a visit to a website, insufficient time to do much reading or obtain much understanding. When put together with the bouncing data it would appear that we are witnessing the emergence of a new form of 'reading' with users 'power browsing' horizontally through sites, titles, contents pages and abstracts in their pursuit of quick wins.

This evidence raises particular questions about what has been traditionally regarded as the 'gold standard' usage metric, the download, which is used by both librarians and publishers in value-for-money and user-satisfaction judgements. It is the e-shopping equivalent of the online purchase. Thus in the case of Elsevier's ScienceDirect website, users spent about 30–40 seconds viewing a full-text article, insufficient time to read an article online. The fact that people are not spending a lot of time online reading content is supported by the fact that the same study showed that people spent relatively more time reading shorter articles online than longer ones. There is a sense that people actually go online to avoid reading, something which is supported by another finding: that, as the length of a paper increases, there is a greater likelihood that it will be viewed as an abstract and less likelihood that the item will be viewed in full text.

So, if people are not reading much online then they must be doing so offline? However, it would be a mistake to believe that everything that is downloaded is actually read or used. Much material is just squirreled away for another day and that day never comes because of a shortage of time and the amount of squirreling that has been done. Also, the online information-seeking process dictates that you print or download first and then take the decision about relevance later, so a good deal of material will be rejected later. The answer to a question that was asked in a CIBER study gave us an idea of the scale on which this happens. Thus *Nucleic Acids* researchers were asked 'Do you always read the full paper before you cite it in your work?' and half of them said it depended and a further 10% said no. These were probably the honest ones! It might be the case that, for many, the only serious reading conducted is of the recreational sort, undertaken on holiday. All the evidence thus suggests that full-text downloads do not actually represent an accurate picture of the extent of reading.

Interestingly, students were shown to be more likely to record long online sessions, those lasting more than 15 minutes, evidence of more substantial online reading, something supported by accompanying questionnaire data. This can be explained partly by personal and generational preferences and is partly to do with the print charges students are faced with in many institutions.

The picture that is building about virtual scholars is that many of them view only a few pages during a visit – a good deal of which are not content pages, a large proportion do not return frequently and the average time spent viewing actual contents indicates that nobody is spending sufficient time online to undertake any significant reading.

It could be said with a high degree of confidence that many librarians and publishers do not design their information systems around this form of user behaviour and how to accommodate it represents their real challenge. The way forward has to be via a flexible, 'suck it and see' model. Trying things out in the digital space and then monitoring for impact and then adjusting accordingly. This is an ongoing process which information providers should have the capability to undertake but to date have shied clear of. Too many sites find themselves stuck in some kind of digital concrete.

6 Diversity

The scholarly audience, always heterogeneous in make-up, has become even more so as scholarly information has become available at everybody's desktop and as a consequence a much wider range of people have been drawn to its products, many of whom would have had very little academic training. We know that even in the case of some quite technical medical sites the informed patient constitutes the majority user group. And we know that it is these new or additional users who bounce more and read less. Log studies also disclose very real differences between the various communities of core users, not just in areas where we might have expected it, like subject field and academic status. Thus significant differences have been found in information seeking according to geographical location, gender, type of organization worked for, whether the user is an author or not, type of university, and attitude towards scholarly communication (Nicholas, Huntington and Jamali, 2007a). What log studies enable us to do is finely gauge the differences in information-seeking behaviour between user communities, meaning that we can avoid hackneyed and simplistic observations of information-seeking behaviour, such as scientists using the most recent material or prefering journal articles. Examples of information-seeking diversity follow, taken from a study of ScienceDirect (www.sciencedirect.com).

Age of material viewed. Scholars from economics (71%), engineering (71%), the social sciences (69%) and computer science (70%) made most views to current (one-year old) material in an online session, whereas material science (51%) and mathematics (52%) users made the least use. There was even a geographical dimension with scholars from East Europe (71%) and Asia (60%) conducting the highest proportion of sessions just viewing current material. By contrast only 19% of African views were to current articles.

Number of journals consulted. Users from material science (39%) and mathematics (38%) were most likely to view two or more journals in a visit. Those from medicine (69%) and computer science (69%) were the most likely to view just one journal.

Return visits (over 5 months). Mathematics users were the most frequent visitors with 41% coming back 15 times or more. Engineers made the least returns, with 54% only making one visit. Repeat visits also increased with age of the user and the number of articles they had published.

Abstract use. The viewing of abstracts tended to increase markedly with the age of the users. About 14% of those aged 36–45 just undertook an abstract only session but this increased to 29% for those aged 56–65 and to 35% of those 65 and over.

Format in which article viewed. Men were far more likely to undertake a PDF only session (37% were so) than women (22%). Chinese users recorded the highest use of PDFs and students made the greatest use of full text (HTML) articles, probably because they are easier to copy and paste.

Searching. Eastern Europeans (47%) and Australians (82%) recorded a high percentage of searches resulting in zero returns. North Americans appeared to be 'successful' searchers – 74% of their searches resulted in one or more matches. However, overall, Germans were the most 'successful' searchers in that they obtained more hits and had fewer zero searches.

Level of activity. Chinese and Germans viewed the greatest number of pages in a session. Students were much more likely to view fewer pages than senior research staff. The number of page views also increased with age.

The OhioLINK studies have shown differences between individual universities and their usage and information-seeking behaviour. This was largely a function of research activity and size of academic community – the more research active and larger the university the higher the activity level.

Much interest is currently focused on one aspect of diversity, that occasioned by age. Chapter 7 examines the information-seeking behaviour of young people in detail but here we shall look at some of the CIBER findings regarding students, something that adds to our understanding of the younger scholar, of course. We have generally found that students constituted the biggest users in terms of sessions and pages viewed, even in the case of e-journal databases which one might have thought were more appropriate to academic staff, largely because they constitute the biggest academic community. There were big subject differences with staff accounting for a high proportion of social science use but a very low proportion of science use. Overall, academic usage declined as academic status increased, which again is unsurprising, given the greater networking opportunities available to senior staff. However, the likelihood of being a heavy user actually increased with academic status. Thus the usage profile of students is that they conduct many sessions but do not view a lot of pages during a session. This is probably a consequence of the directed nature of much of their searching and their preference for using internet search engines which produce many false links; this all fits the picture of students as 'bouncers'. However, it has to be said that this finding is largely based on e-journal use and it turned out not to be the case with e-books, where students viewed more pages in a session than staff. This is explained by the fact that e-books are a more appropriate form of e-resource to students, so they would naturally make more heavy use of the resource. Students were more likely to record long online (reading) sessions lasting more than 15 minutes, evidence, perhaps, of substantial online reading, something which was borne out by associated questionnaire data. Students were much more likely to read online than other academic groups and this is partly to do with personal preference and partly to do with print charges students are faced with in many institutions.

It is clear given the level of diversity that has been demonstrated, a one-size-fits-all policy from information providers is not going to be effective and that there exists as much (albeit, still largely unacknowledged) diversity in the existing scholarly population as is likely to exist between today's scholars and tomorrow's, yet policy-makers tend not to fret about this. Without such detailed or niche information it is impossible to target services and determine scholarly outcomes.

7 Checking

Much store is set by librarians on authority and trust, with the belief that scholars need it and they and their systems offer it — see for instance the marketing of gateway sites, like Intute, which portray themselves as a safe haven from the information wild west that is the web. However, in cyberspace authority is not easily ascribed because there are so many players involved and judgements about trust and authority are not so easily made. And here lies a very big problem for libraries. Take the example of virtual researchers searching from their office in a university. They have conducted a Google search, as increasingly large numbers of them do, to find the

Synergy database. On connection a cookie identifies them and provides them with full-text access. Now these researchers used a Microsoft Browser, then Google, then Synergy, then arrived at the *Journal of Computer-Mediated Communication* and on inspection alighted on an article by David Brown from City University. Throw into the pot that they might or might not have known that the library had paid the subscription, so providing full-text access; or that Synergy is produced by Blackwell and that the journal was published on behalf of the International Communication Association. In these circumstances where does the authority lie? This is very, very difficult to determine.

The evidence in fact tells us that many users are promiscuous, assess authority and determine trust very quickly (in a matter of seconds) by cross-checking and long experience (bouncing tells us this) and if they notice kite marks, assurance labels and the like, they only do this fleetingly. There just are not the strong brand names there which help the e-shopper. Furthermore, the younger they are the less trusting (and more promiscuous) they are, and less likely to recognize traditional brand names. Indeed, for some, Google is a far stronger virtual brand than Synergy and if they thought that Synergy was in fact part of the Google family, they would probably trust it more than if they knew it came from Wiley-Blackwell, and that it was a publisher. Authority (and relevance) has to be won (and checked) and at present, unfortunately, we have little evidence regarding the authority a library possesses in cyberspace, although the aforementioned study of BL Learning appears to suggest that the BL is a recognized information brand in the USA. Libraries, like the British Library, have set up camp on Facebook and other social networking sites, cognizant that if you are not certain of your brand or presence, it might be possible to enhance this by association.

The walled-garden approaches being adopted by publishers, like OUP, who have genuine brand and authority claims, might prove more successful with the consumer. Thus with e-textbooks, e-monographs, e-journals and e-reference works being bundled together in some publisher's offerings it might be the publisher who will provide the authoritative information experience, in the case of OUP, the Oxford experience.

8 Access expectation

The SuperBook study highlighted a new feature of scholarly information seeking, and that is the differences in information-seeking profile between on-site and off-site users of the same service, in this case in regard to Oxford Scholarship Online. Two-thirds of UCL usage took place on site. Off-site users differed from on-site users in that they adopted a more direct approach by zeroing in on content, undertaking less navigating. Thus three-quarters of their views were to full-text pages; by comparison the figure for on-site users was just over a half. Off-site viewers were also more likely to view an e-book in a session (users could just look at the homepage or help pages), with only 1 in 10 sessions not recording a view to a book, as compared to 4 in 10 for on-site users – a significant difference.

The explanation for this could be that in the relatively early days of e-book access which they found themselves in, external users did not expect to find the material free; they had a negative access expectation, and were eager to grab the opportunity to view or squirrel away more pages. By contrast, those people searching from within UCL had a positive access expectation; they expected the service to be around for the foreseeable future and there was therefore no pressure to download straightaway.

9 Robotic

What brings home more than anything else that huge changes have occurred in the scholarly information landscape is the fact that, for many websites, robots and mechanical agents, used extensively to index web content, account for around half of their usage. This was true of both the BL Learning and Intute sites, and the journal *Glycobiology*. In the case of some more rarefied AHRC-funded websites the figure is closer to 90%! Proprietary software tends to underestimate robot use because some robots, in order to obtain extensive access to the site, masquerade themselves as humans and do not present themselves as robots – for instance, by moving slowly and restricting the volume of information they view. Of course, robot use while not being human can be a factor in humans finding the site, as in the case of robots that index sites for search engines. So we know that the robot is the majority scholarly user, and that most sites underestimate their usage, but beyond that we really do not know what to do with this finding!

10 Internationality

There are no geographical boundaries in the virtual information space and scholars seek out information (and brands) internationally and UK brands appear to be in high demand from overseas users in the scholarly field. This could be to do with the perceived high quality of UK education. We have also learned earlier that users from different countries seek information often in very different ways. This is what one might have expected but perhaps the scale of it is really surprising, and in some cases possibly 'embarrassing' as we shall learn. This is best illustrated by reference to CIBER studies of the British Library's learning site for young scholars and Intute, a JISC-sponsored scholarly gateway site. In both cases the UK audience was a minority one and US scholars were the majority user group, as we found to be the case with *The Times* five years earlier. Thus with regard to Intute the US accounted for 35% of sessions while the UK accounted for 29%; Europe accounted for 10% and Asia 12%. Clearly this has big implications for national governments, in this specific case the UK government. What will the tax payer say if they learn that Government money is going to help the Americans become better and more informed searchers?

Another good example of the international usage of scholarly sources comes from an evaluation of the OUP published journal, *Glycobiology*, a journal which publishes both subscriber (regular) and open access (OA) articles (Figure 6.4 overleaf). Most use of OA and subscriber articles came from Asia and the USA. Use from the UK, the journal's home country, was very low indeed. OA articles proved particularly attractive for Asian users.

11 Currency and current awareness

Clearly users are interested in the new but this has been exaggerated by a number of factors. Older material was always more difficult to access (back files are the last things to go online) and the early retrieval systems like those

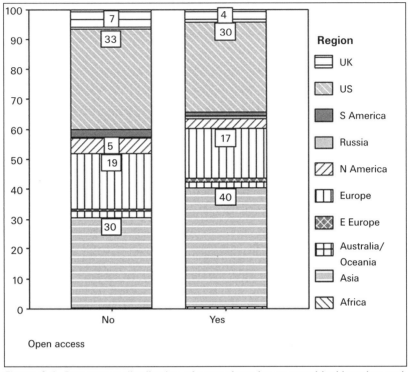

Figure 6.4 Percentage distribution of page views by geographical location and type of article view for the journal *Glycobiology*

used by Dialog prioritized the viewing of the most recent first (a reverse chronological display was the default); as all Google users know we make our selections from the first few screens, which means that new material is much more likely to be viewed. This is a powerful example of the huge impact of digital visibility on usage in a very large and crowded information space. This has led to researchers reporting that the most recent year (or two) of a journal accounts for the vast majority of uses, despite the fact that journal might have a back file of 30 years or more. However, massive improvements in access to back files and search engines that prioritize relevance over age have increased the visibility of older material and this shows up quite strongly in the logs. The figures are quite astonishing. Thus in the case of OhioLINK, even in scientific areas where currency might be thought to be held at a high premium, there was substantial use of the back file. Thus articles older than five years of age accounted for 31% of page views in materials science and meteorology. The figure was 33% in the case of psychology and psychiatry. In fact, the only field in which the current year attracted the majority of all use was in genetics, where 55% of use was accounted for by that year. This finding has had publishers scurrying to buy back the rights to their back files.

Of course, as expected, the picture for e-books shows even less concentration in the new. Thus, in the case of Oxford Scholarship Online, with strong coverage in the arts, humanities and social sciences, the most recent two years accounted for just 17% of views (25% of the books available were that old). The possible reasons for this are:

- students, a major user group for e-books, are not so preoccupied with the new
- it takes time to become an accepted textbook or monograph
- lecturers are poor at updating readings
- social science/humanities titles do not obsolesce as much.

This takes us nicely to the topic of current awareness which so fascinated LIS researchers in the 1960s and 1970s, partly because of the problems in dealing with information overload which was the result of the information explosion (another phrase nobody uses today). SDI or selective dissemination of information, which was a regularly pushed information service based upon author-supplied keywords that represented ongoing interests, was thought to be the solution then. However, logs and focus groups tell us that current awareness is no longer a discrete or regular activity. Instead, people tend to update themselves when the need arises; it is a problem-driven and not a time-driven event any more, if indeed, it ever was. In fact, currency generally does not seem to raise the concerns it might have done just ten years ago. Presumably this is because currency is no longer a big problem, the information tap is now always in the on-position. Users do seem though to appreciate the benefits of obtaining early intelligence through pre-prints and in this respect ScienceDirect's practice has been commended by a number of people we have spoken to. Conference attendance is also seen as an enjoyable and convenient way of keeping up to date with key developments. Mention has already been made of the benefits of making working papers available online because of the currency gains.

12 Interdisciplinary

Commentators and researchers in the information field have long been interested in the extent to which researchers use the literatures of other disciplines, and whether subject literatures are self-contained or not. The ScienceDirect investigation provided an opportunity to explore this in more detail in the huge virtual space where the opportunities for interdisciplinary searching are greater, it being much easier to range more widely in search of relevant material. Figure 6.5 provides an analysis of the subject of journals used by the self-proclaimed subject credentials of the user. What it generally shows is that researchers do range, quite widely, and with some frequency. Physics proved to be the most 'insular' field, with 71% of those describing themselves as physicists having viewed physics journals during a search

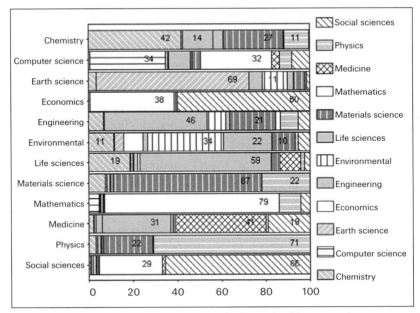

Figure 6.5 Percentage breakdown of use by journal subject grouping across user subject group for ScienceDirect

session. Environmental and computer scientists were least likely just to view journals within their discipline, just a third did so. Computer science users were just as likely to view mathematical journals as their own, while environmental scientists were heavy users of life science journals.

E-book evidence from the Oxford Scholarship Online study proved equally illuminating. Users accessing via biochemistry and gene sub-networks (another way that the user's subject can be established) mainly looked at philosophy pages, which demonstrates how, when book content is opened up, this encourages user's from other fields to take the mouth-size information bites that they require. On the other hand, perhaps unsurprisingly, users on the philosophy sub-network viewed only philosophy titles.

13 Scatter

A long-known characteristic of information-seeking behaviour is that a relatively small number of the titles available account for a relatively high proportion of use. This is also true of the virtual environment but what is different here is that the massive audience and increased access has meant that for all titles usage is boosted, so much so that titles once out of print are now back in print, boosted by the 'long user tail' and print-on-demand facilities. This is best illustrated in the case of OhioLINK, where all bar five of the 6800 titles available were used within the 15-month survey period. Nevertheless there was the inevitable concentration in use (Nicholas, Huntington, Jamali and Tenopir, 2006a, b). Thus, 5% of journals accounted for well over a third (38%) of usage, 10% accounted for approximately half of usage (53%), and half of all journals accounted for about 93% of use. We can conclude from this that virtually all journals were used, but that half of all journals accounted for only 7% of use.

Table 6.6 shows the classic ranked analysis much favoured by information science researchers; in this case it is a ranking of the most used journals on OhioLINK.

Table 6.6 Top 25 OhioLINK journals by usage – estimated figures (October 2004)

Title	Total use
The Lancet	4662
Journal of Personality and Social Psychology	4315
Angewandte Chemie International Edition	3918
Reference Services Review	3708
The Journal of Academic Librarianship	3258
Automatica	3250
Biochemical and Biophysical Research Communications	3076
American Psychologist	3036
Journal of Advanced Nursing	2904
Library Hi Tech	2902
Social Science and Medicine	2862
Journal of Business Ethics	2853
American Journal of Medical Genetics	2825
Journal of the American Chemical Society	2636
Journal of Molecular Biology	2625
Tetrahedron Letters	2581
Early Childhood Education Journal	2528
Journal of the American Dietetic Association	2517
Government Information Quarterly	2446
Portal Libraries and the Academy	2432
Journal of the American College of Cardiology	2421
Journal of Government Information	2317
Analytical Chemistry	2202
Child Development	2199
Personality and Social Psychology Bulletin	2194

Unpicking the OhioLINK scatter data a little more: during October 2004 it was estimated that 319,049 full-text articles were viewed and of these 247,612 were separate articles (Nicholas and Huntington, 2006). The study found no evidence that use was dominated by a small number of articles – a common misconception. The top 25 articles viewed accounted for just over half (0.64) a percent of article views. The most popular paper accounted for 0.14% of article views. Most articles were just viewed once. Nearly three-quarters (72%) of articles were viewed once, 25% were viewed between 2 and 4 times, about 1.5% were viewed between 5 and 10 times and just 0.5% of articles were viewed 11 or more times.

Impacts on information seeking

Access is not the barrier it once was, and open access and institutional repository initiatives are improving things for the disenfranchized, those not part of academe and big deal arrangements. Overload as mentioned earlier is prevalent but users see it as an acceptable trade-off for unbelievable levels of access – 24/7, and from virtually anywhere thanks to wireless and Athens authentication. The searching process, once delegated to intermediaries, is thought now to be easy, thanks to Google and its like. However, the logs do point to enough failure at the terminal, especially among the young and non-core users, to suggest that search skills and levels of digital literacy are a (unacknowledged) problem for quite large numbers of people. Time is clearly a barrier still, but the ability to be able to work from home or the train has masked this somewhat. Here we shall concentrate on the impacts that are on everybody's lips at the present moment, the hot topics, Web 2.0 and open access publishing.

Chapter 7 examines Web 2.0 in more detail as it is expected that Web 2.0 facilities will prove more attractive to young users, primed by their experiences of social networking sites. Here we shall just concentrate on its impact on information-seeking behaviour and test some of the assumptions being made by Web 2.0 advocates.

Some commentators believe that there could be generational disconnect with Facebook, etc. users in their teens and twenties, whose brains are still going through significant development, and that this will have big implications for scholarly information providers:

> Facebook does seem to produce a genuinely different perspective on trusted sources, the right of peers to arbitrate social interactions and the frequency and triviality of communication. Could this translate into a fundamentally different hardwiring of the brain – as much as such a thing can exist – once adulthood is reached? This kind of collective brain remapping has happened often in the past (moving from hunter gathering to farming, farming to urban, industrial life, etc.), but rarely with such rapidity.
>
> (Cookson, 2008)

Cognizant of this and witnessing the astonishing success of Facebook and YouTube with the young (and not so young) and worried about the relevance of their 'traditional' services to the young, many librarians have gone down the social networking route. In an attempt to adapt to a perceived change in information-seeking behaviour, sites have set up blogs and other kinds of social and interactive facilities. It is clearly early days yet but we have found that such services only account for a very small proportion of use; most people very much concentrate on mainstream, traditional bibliographic activities. A no-frills service is what seems to be required. Thus in the case of the Intute service, the blog only accounted for about 0.5% of pages viewed. However this did represent 10,000 views a month and they did prove attractive to certain types of user. Thus blogs had a special appeal for US users.

Interestingly at the very time we are writing this chapter it is being reported that the number of (British) Facebook users has fallen for the first time, monthly unique visitors are down by 5% (Sherwin, 2008). This is put down to two factors: Facebook fatigue – users are finding that managing their virtual life is too demanding and that the sheer amount of information updates causes strains; also 'social networking is as much about who isn't on the site as who is'. When libraries, museums and the like start profiles its 'cool' brand is devalued. MySpace and Bebo visits are down too.

Web 2.0 is generally a difficult subject to do justice to because older researchers feel constrained in their criticisms by the fact that these developments are associated with the Google Generation, youth generally, and represent a dumbing down in information seeking. Thus at a focus group attended by the authors, comprised largely of senior researchers, the idea that an e-journal database should adopt Web 2.0 facilities went down like a lead balloon. They could not see the need for this or how people had the time to indulge in what they clearly thought were side-show activities. There is enough to do without engaging in blogs, wikis, RSS and the like was the general message coming from the group.

Added-value activities have always played a minor part in the usage of databases as CIBER research has shown. This is partly because the core service is so appreciated. It is also partly because the percentages used mask the real volumes of activity that are undertaken in regard to added value services. E-mail alerts however do appear to be widely appreciated.

Open access publishing (and institutional repositories) is busy making the contents of journals more accessible by making them free to the user. It would be expected that this would lead to even higher volumes of journal usage, because clearly there is a widespread belief that cost is an obstacle to journal use; CIBER are currently (on behalf of OUP) testing this assertion. Early data from the journal *Glycobiology*, which publishes articles in both open access and subscriber form, appear to support the assertion. Articles published in an open access (OA) form attracted far more use, sometimes as much as three times the usage of articles under subscriber control. However, while the OA articles attracted more views, they were viewed for a shorter time. This could be due to what we have noticed elsewhere, a squirreling form of behaviour. That is, users download the articles while they are free, just in case this state is a temporary one. It could be of course that the shorter time could signify that the articles are not so highly rated. Interestingly, what distorts the picture somewhat is the (widely prevalent) practice of self-use of articles, authors and their institutions downloading their own articles – something that is easier to do with OA articles.

With the greater access afforded by OA it might also be expected that more use would come from outside of academe, where the Big Deals already provide comprehensive access to journals. This proved to be the case and users viewing OA articles were more likely to come from net-providers and commercial organizations and less likely to come from academic organizations.

Outcomes

We have looked extensively at how people navigate and view their way around the virtual scholarly space. However, as we know, that is simply a means to an end, and it is the end we should be concerned with, because that is what concerns consumers and those that provide and finance the space in which they conduct their activities. To begin with the benefits of online information access were measured in terms of the extent of that access – the more access the better. The medium was not just the message but also the outcome – but no longer: people are beginning to question what all the activity means. There is loads of activity, but maybe much of it is 'drowning man stuff', terrain viewing rather than real reading and learning. Lots of hits are just searchers passing through; they put in the wrong word and went to the wrong place. This raises big questions about impacts and the place of digital literacy.

In fact there is a dearth of information on the academic outcomes of providing the academic community with unprecedented levels of access to e-journals and e-books; whether, for instance, it has led to an improvement in the research process and outcomes and how this varies for types of institution and user. The assumption – made by librarians, publishers and academics – is naturally that increased and enhanced access is beneficial and that the most research-active researchers are also the most proficient and effective users of the literature. To date nobody has sought to establish this in an evidence-based way, in regard to diverse subjects and institutions and on a national scale. It might be because people fear the answer. However, without these data it makes it very difficult to persuade university vice chancellors and provosts to continue spending, and in a world awash with information which is easily accessible and perceived to be free or cheap they are proving harder to convince.

CIBER are currently involved in a Research Information Network study (www.publishing.ucl.ac.uk/ejournals.html) which seeks to attach outcomes to information-seeking behaviour for a selection of UK universities and Government research laboratories. Usage will be monitored and mapped for a select number of departments. For each of the case study departments we will create group productivity and citation impact metrics and compare these with a range of information behaviour indicators obtained from the deep log analysis (e.g. levels of activity, search/navigational approach). Online techniques will be used to capture publications lists (from Thomson ISI) for each department for the period 2006–8 and then to generate production curves (cumulative authors v. cumulated papers) for each department as well as for the discipline as a whole. This will facilitate a simple visualization of the group productivity of each department relative to its disciplinary norm. From those curves will be generated an indicator, a Herfindhal index, which will summarize a department's relative productivity: a value of 100 would mean that the group is completely average for the discipline; 120, that it is 20% more productive, and so on.

Citation impact will be measured using another new CIBER concept: the virtual impact factor. What this means is that the entire output of a department will be treated as though it were a 'virtual journal' in its own right, thus enabling easy comparison with the discipline. This data will again be presented as an index, with 100 representing average citation performance for the discipline. The way that these indicators are constructed means that valid comparisons can be made between different disciplines.

This will prove to be a very useful exercise in terms of starting to investigate what relationships there might be between how researchers use online journals and the value that this brings to their research. It will certainly raise issues and questions for a qualitative research strand which will seek to explain what we find in the logs and output metrics. This would enable us to identify best practice and start answering the question on many people's lips: whether top flight research groups use e-journals differently (for example lower bouncing rates, longer session averages).

Conclusions

This is the first time that we have presented a full and complete description of our model of information seeking in a digital environment. And one can see that this is a very different model than those produced in a largely pre-digital information environment, upon which many people still base their information activities, strategies and services. Why should it be so different?

Firstly, the web has caused people to behave in quite a new way with regard to information. This would seem to contradict accepted ideas of evolutionary biology/psychology that basic human behaviour does not change suddenly. However it is generally agreed that we have never seen change on this scale and rapidity before so this could well be the case. Also in some cases it is not so much a new form of behaviour, rather a much more virulent strain of that behaviour. Thus, presumably, people power-browsed abstract services before, but not on a global scale. Secondly, people are behaving in the same way that they always did, but now we can see their true behaviour, which previously we could not. Thirdly, people behave in the same way as before, and this way was noticed before, but not accepted, because it did not match the way people 'should' behave. This would seem to be the least likely of the explanations but might possibly be shown to be so by an analysis of the 'information user' literature of, say, the 1970s, before anything resembling the web came into being.

We shall now conclude by examining the realities and challenges of what we have discovered: the sheer enormity of the change that has occurred to information seeking as a result of the digital transition; the problems arising from the change; the implications of the change for information providers; the likely impact of e-books on information seeking; the scholarly information marketplace; the growth of the amateur scholar; the significance of the e-shopper.

The enormity of the change

What brings home the enormity of the changes that have occurred is who would ever have thought, say ten years ago even, that half of the users of any scholarly information resource would be robots, that of those that were human, a majority would dip in and out in a matter of seconds, and that of those that did not, a majority would be foreign? Surely no one, these are salutary and unusual times! Nor would we have expected to find that the majority of academic staff in the sciences and social science had deserted the library for their desktops, the coffee bar or railway carriage. As one researcher said at a recent focus group discussing the information seeking of researchers, 'libraries are empty nowadays'. They also said that they had not been near the place for three years, and they said this with no sense of guilt, just a sense of realism.

The digital transition has been a big success, but there are casualties

Scholars appear to have taken to the new digital information environment with some alacrity and have taken full advantage of the huge digital choice that is offered to them. And we can refute claims that it is simply the author and his or her mother who are using the resource, although we have come across cases where the author (and colleagues) has clearly inflated his or her hit counts – in the case of the journal *Glycobiology*, for instance. There is, however, some possibly disturbing evidence that much use appears to be passing and/or ineffectual, and could possibly constitute a 'dumbing down' in information-seeking behaviour; enough evidence to make us reflect on the effectiveness of information literacy strategy and programmes. It would indeed be ironic if the web that provided for the enfranchisement of the user in information terms was also guilty of the disenfranchisement of whole swathes of the population, because they have not been able to take advantage of the information deluge.

Implications for information providers

Everything and everyone in the scholarly landscape is changing at a rapid rate of knots and the various user communities that inhabit the space are responding to this in diverse ways. And the only way of keeping in touch and relevant is by monitoring and evaluating their usage, but the COUNTER data most libraries feed off only records the use of material and not the types of people who are using the material, and no university that we know has a department devoted to this work, say, a department of user studies. Yet we all know it is consumers who are calling the shots, so why keep them at arm's length?

Fantastic access, huge digital choice and a common/multifunction retrieval platform are changing everything; scholars are now consumers in every sense of the word and they are exercising their new-found powers and wings to take their custom to whomever they feel best meets their needs. This is transforming their relationship with all information providers, and most notably with that of the library. Without the necessary user or market data and general day-to-day contact with users, the response of libraries has tended to be a technological, rather than a user, one and it is looking as though this is going to be a big, big mistake. How many commentators have said this in the past and yet we are still saying it today? However, the stakes are much higher now and the risks of complete melt-down never more real. Forget technological innovation for now, instead there needs to be a wholesale questioning of the assumptions made about today's information-enfranchised scholar and, as we have demonstrated in this chapter, a very good start can be made through the collection and analysis of the user data (logs) that are so abundantly being produced by digital information systems, remotely and without massive effort. The future is now and instead of looking ahead (almost as an escape from current dilemmas) we should be looking at what is happening now, employing the deep log tools so readily on offer to do this.

E-books – a tipping point

Prospects might already be looking dim but the introduction of e-books could be catastrophic for librarians. Thus the expected popularity of e-books will come with an as yet unknown price for university libraries. Firstly, because this will mean that more people will not have to visit the library. Academic libraries tend to occupy an enormous amount of premium space in universities and this space is largely filled by books and students. Provide access to the relatively small number of books that students need in their dorms, bars and recreational space and who would bet against a huge drop in library visits? Something, of course, which will then lead to questions being asked about whether the library needs all the space it occupies. Secondly, while the advent of e-books in numbers will mean libraries will become more remote from their users, it will also mean that publishers will become ever closer, because they will have all the knowledge as to how the user behaves – the users' footfalls take place increasingly in their virtual space. Furthermore, they can offer the products directly to the user. Indeed, with e-textbooks, e-monographs, e-journals and e-reference works being bundled together in some publishers' offerings it might be the publisher who will provide the e-library experience. Sounds like the changing of the guard to us – who would bet against this happening, publishers have the brand and own content.

There could be a difference here in regard to the Google Generation – current scholars will have had long contact with libraries and be more likely to make the association with libraries and information provision, but the Google Generation will arrive on the scholarly scene without the memory.

The scholarly information marketplace

The very strong consumer traits that operate in what was once thought of as a conservative, staid scholarly information market and the huge consumer demand for the product has been clearly established by CIBER research. There is now enough data – and confidence in the data – to start asking where this should be taking information professionals and how it can be used to improve the scholarly communication system, which sometimes resembles a battleground. However, the moment we do this, we run into a major obstacle and that is that we do not have a true consumer market/mechanism, and this distorts, frustrates and creates a myriad of problems for the user-consumer (and information professional, for that matter). What is really needed is a major market re-alignment to take cognizance of the consumer revolution that has taken place. Thus, while academic information consumers have a choice, albeit partly dependent upon the wealth of their own particular university, they do not really have a real or free choice because librarians largely make choices for them in that they determine which journals they get for free and which ones they do not (and as we have mentioned earlier many users are not aware of the choices being made). It does not help either that librarians are not always very effective at employing the available usage data to ensure their choices are indeed the ones the consumers would make themselves. Indeed, OhioLINK data has shown that when consumers are given a choice they often make different choices from the acquisition librarians.

The market is in fact further distorted by the consumer. Thus, in the case of the digital journals to which they have free access, they are clearly not obliged to exercise any discretion over what they consume (download), in the way that shoppers are by the hit their credit card takes. Librarians are not inclined to intervene since what they actually want is to show that big deals and the like, which they pay upfront for, deliver lots of downloads.

We have argued elsewhere (Nicholas, Huntington, Dobrowski et al., 2007, 185) that the best solution would be:

to give consumers what they actually want – full and largely unfettered choice; let them make the decisions about what they want to spend the money on, but at the same time make sure they are responsible in their decision making. Thus, for instance, they could be given so many download electronic credits by the library (or similar agency) at the beginning of each term, with a different tariff, maybe, for postgraduates, science students, and professors. These electronic credits could be accepted by any scholarly journal vendors – e-commerce has long ago sorted out the mechanics by which this can be done. Where the virtual scholar chooses to spend them is up to them, they could – and we have evidence already that they would – shop around.

The amateur scholar

With information now available in their own home that a national library would have been proud of a few years ago and liberated from the tyranny of having to pay for information or beg access to a decent library, it can come as no surprise that so many of the general public have joined the army of virtual scholars. Everyone has an interest of some kind and people today are encouraged by the media and government to comment on current issues (by e-mail or phone-in). We are all scholars and experts now and have a library of immense power at our beck and call. These people have been labelled the disenfranchised (by librarians) because they do not have full-text access to information and 'turnaways' or 'noise' by publishers (they are turned away because they do not have subscriber access, or clutter up their sites looking for an offer or a lead). As we have seen they are large in number and are fuelling a lot of the growth in scholarly information consumption; to them open access publishing is a real bonus.

The e-shopper

We have mentioned a number of times how the digital information seeker behaves in a similar fashion to the e-shopper and this is why we have an e-shopper chapter in the book. This point could not have been made clearer than in a study of Emerald (www.emeraldinsight.com) where users exhibited what could only be described as a sales mentality. In the way that shoppers are easily swayed in their choice by 'offers', so too are database users. Thus, on the Emerald site, once a week the articles from two journals were offered for free. What happened was that for these two journals – whatever they were – use jumped immediately by a factor of ten, only to drop down again to pre-offer levels once the promotion was over. Clearly it was not just the fact that the journals were 'free' that fuelled use but it also has something to do with the enhanced digital visibility that these journals were given at the time by the very fact they were part of a promotion. An analysis of download times before and after free weeks suggested that a squirreling (or access expectation) behaviour was being witnessed. It transpired that download times in free weeks were much shorter, suggesting people were simply storing for a later day, rather than 'reading' at the time. This is the same behavioural trait we have noted off-campus e-book users displaying.

The adage 'we are all librarians now' was once used to highlight the fact that thanks to the internet everyone has access to vast stores of information. This adage should however now be replaced by a far more pertinent one, 'we are all consumers now', in recognition of the fact that we have not adopted the behavioural traits of the traditional librarian but those of the shopper.

References

CIBER (2008) *The Information Behaviour of the Researcher of the Future*, www.publishing.ucl.ac.uk/download/GoogleGeneration.pdf.

Cookson, R. (2008) The Google Generation, e-mail sent on 2 June.

Ellis, D. and Haugan, M. (1997) Modelling the Information-Seeking Patterns of Engineers and Research Scientists in an Industrial Environment, *Journal of Documentation*, **53** (4), 384–403.

Naughton, J. (2008) Thanks, Gutenberg – but We're Too Pressed for Time to Read, *The Guardian*, (27 January), www.guardian.co.uk/media/2008/jan/27/internet.pressandpublishing.

Nicholas, D. and Huntington, P. (2006) Electronic Journals: are they really used?, *Interlending & Document Supply*, **34** (2), 74–7.

Nicholas, D., Huntington, P., Dobrowolski, T. and Rowlands, I. (2007) Creating a

Consumer Market for Scholarly Journals, *Interlending & Document Supply*, **35** (4), 184–6.

Nicholas, D., Huntington, P. and Jamali, H. R. (2007a) Diversity in the Information-Seeking Behaviour of the Virtual Scholar: institutional comparisons, *Journal of Academic Librarianship*, **33** (6), 21–38.

Nicholas, D., Huntington, P. and Jamali, H. R. (2007b) Open Access in Context: a user study, *Journal of Documentation*, **63** (6), 853–78.

Nicholas, D., Huntington, P. and Jamali, H. R. (2008) User Diversity: as demonstrated by deep log analysis, *Electronic Library*, **26** (1), 21–38.

Nicholas, D., Huntington, P., Jamali, H. R. and Tenopir, C. (2006a) Finding Information in (Very Large) Digital Libraries: a deep log approach to determining differences in use according to method of access, *Journal of Academic Librarianship*, **32** (2), 119–26.

Nicholas, D., Huntington, P., Jamali, H. R. and Tenopir, C. (2006b) OhioLINK – Ten Years On: what deep log analysis tells us about the impact of Big Deals, *Journal of Documentation*, **62** (4) July 2006, 482–508.

Nicholas, D., Huntington, P., Jamali, H. R. and Williams, P. (2007) *Digital Health Information for the Consumer: evidence and policy implications*, Ashgate.

Nicholas, D., Huntington, P., Lievesley, N. and Wasti, A. (2000) Evaluating Consumer Web Site Logs: case study, *The Times/Sunday Times* website, *Journal of Information Science*, **26** (6), 399–411.

Nicholas, D., Huntington, P., Rowlands, I., Dobrowolski, T. and Jamali, H. R. (2007) SuperBook: an action research project, *Online Information 2007 Proceedings*, 50–7.

Nicholas, D., Williams, P. and Dennis, K. (2004) Improving Websites in the Voluntary Sector, *Library & Information Update*, CILIP: the Chartered Institute of Library and Information Professionals, **3** (3), 35–7.

Peters, T. A. (2001) What's the Big Deal?, *Journal of Academic Librarianship*, **27** (4), 302–4.

Sherwin, A. (2008) Web Socialites Succumb to Facebook Fatigue, *The Times*, (22 February), 10.

Wilson, T. D. (1999) Models in Information-Seeking Behaviour Research, *Journal of Documentation*, **55** (3), 249–70.

7

The 'Google Generation' – myths and realities about young people's digital information behaviour

PETER WILLIAMS
IAN ROWLANDS
MAGGIE FIELDHOUSE

Summary

This chapter looks at the scholar of the future by considering what we know currently about the information-seeking behaviour of today's young people and how their practices may impact on the role of information providers and the delivery mechanisms they put in place. First, however, it attempts to debunk some myths that have grown up around the so-called 'Google Generation'. Next, it examines the literature on information search behaviour, information evaluation skills, the social web, and young people's use of libraries, to establish what is known about young people's information seeking. Finally, it discusses the information literacy agenda and the policy implications emerging from the current 'state of play'. The chapter's main findings are that much popular writing overestimates the impact of ICTs on the young, and that the ubiquitous presence of technology in their lives has not resulted in improved information retrieval or evaluation skills. It concludes that these skills need to be developed during formative school years – remedial information literacy programmes at university level are likely to be ineffective. Concerted action between libraries, schools and parents is recommended.

Introduction

When we talk about the future of libraries, newspapers, books, digital broadcasting and education, we often ignore one of the most important aspects. We tend to focus on information delivery and not on the nature of information seeking. The internet is clearly revolutionizing information delivery, but what are its impacts on information seeking, especially among younger internet users? The subject of this chapter is the scholar of the future and what we know, at what may be considered to be a very early stage in the internet revolution, about the information-seeking behaviour of young people and how this may impact on the role of information providers and their delivery mechanisms.

Marshall McLuhan developed the notion of the Gutenberg Galaxy in the early 1960s to describe a universe, based on the advent of the printed book, of linear exposition, quiet contemplation, disciplined reading and study (McLuhan, 1962). How are young people reacting to not only a profound change in the way that information is delivered, but also to the new kinds of information that the internet has brought into our homes, schools and colleges? Is the Gutenberg Galaxy still intact or is it about to be deconstructed? These are very big questions, and the intention of this chapter is rather modest by comparison: simply to outline what we actually know about the information behaviour of young scholars and any indications of technology-induced change.

Most academic studies examine the behaviour of contemporary cohorts of young people (e.g. Agosto, 2002, 2006; Borgman et al., 1995) without comparing their results with those accrued historically. As a result, it is not easy to establish trends in young people's information behaviour over time. There is also a dearth of research comparing age groups, and those studies that do (e.g. Shenton and Dixon, 2003a, 2003b, 2003c, 2004) tend to focus on those within the usual range of general education, rather than comparing teenagers with people in their late twenties or thirties. The end result is that we have many major gaps in the evidence base, but not so many as to justify some of the extreme claims made about the Google Generation in recent months and years.

Some Google Generation myths exploded

Later in this chapter, we will present a detailed review of what we do actually
know about the information behaviour of young people today. Before we do
this, it is important to tackle some of the myths that have sprung up around
the Google Generation. Popular discourse, as represented in the media,
sadly including the library trade press, claims that the current generation is
something very different indeed from its forebears.

Three general assumptions are made in this discourse, which all seem to
be highly suspect. First, the assumption, implied by the very label 'Google
Generation', that today's youngsters can reasonably be considered as a
homogeneous body. Second, that they are all equipped with the latest
gadgetry: iPod, laptop, mobile phone connected to the internet, etc. and
have been brought up in an immersive ICT environment. None of the
research we have looked at discusses young people who do not wish to be
surrounded by technology or do not have the resources to do so, yet they
clearly exist. Third, there is an assumption that the students are
overwhelmingly dedicated to studying (see e.g. Gardner and Eng, 2005) and
are happy to invest time exploring sources for the most appropriate
information in order to carry out their assignments. As described later, there
is much evidence to question each of these assumptions.

For the remainder of this section, we identify seven popular Google
Generation myths and expose them to closer scrutiny and, in many cases,
counter argument.

1 The Google Generation prefers visual information over text.
(e.g. Kipnis and Childs, 2005)

There is certainly a strong liking for the visual, but text is still very influential
in conveying information (the popularity of texting even over voice testifies
to this). The underlying assumption, that reading is eschewed these days in
favour of computers, videogames, digital music players, video cams, cell
phones, 'and all the other toys and tools of the digital age' (Prensky, 2001,
unpaginated), is questionable.

In fact, there is evidence that young people are reading more than previously, despite the additional attractions vying for their attention. The BBC cites (as yet unpublished) research from Dale Southerton of the University of Manchester, that:

> Young people in the UK are reading more than they did a quarter of a century
> ago. . . . while Britons spent just three minutes a day on average reading a
> book in 1975, by 2000 this rose to seven minutes. And when magazines and
> newspapers were taken into account, Britons were reading five minutes more
> every day in 2000, compared to their 1970s counterparts.
>
> (Rodgers, 2007, unpaginated)

The news that young people are still reading should not be so surprising when one considers the 'Harry Potter phenomenon'. Despite the mammoth effort required to read these tomes, sales have been enormous, with more than two million copies sold in the UK of *Harry Potter and the Half-Blood Prince* in the first 24 hours of its release (BBC Online, 2005).

A 2005 survey of over 8,000 primary and secondary pupils in England found that

> half the sample of pupils said they enjoy reading either very much or quite a
> lot and rated themselves as proficient readers. The majority of pupils read
> every day or once/twice a week. . . . Pupils generally held positive attitudes
> towards reading – agreeing with statements that reading is important and
> disagreeing with statements that reading is boring, hard, or for girls rather than
> boys.   (Clarke and Foster, 2005, 2)

Even when electronic media are considered, there is some evidence that text is not being eschewed by young users, simply because information may be presented in other ways. Apart from studies by Fidel et al. (1999) and Large et al. (1998) that find children opting for textual information in order to complete their homework more effectively, Loh and Williams (2002) show that text may be as interesting to children as other media even when there is no pressure to complete school work. They looked at children's perceptions of web design elements and features they considered 'cool'. The researchers concluded that 'content was more important for children than presentation; the novelty colour, sound, and animation may initially draw children to a website, but after the novelty effect faded, it was interesting content that motivated children to return to the site' (quoted in Large, Beheshti and Breuleux, 1998, 364).

2 The Google Generation demands a variety of learning experiences and is used to being entertained. (Kipnis and Childs, 2005; Hay, 2000)

Information media must be interesting or they will fail to be used to their full potential, which is simply to restate the above in a slightly different way and to expose it as a tautology. Some library commentators argue that games technologies, for example, should be used to engage users in new and exciting ways. However, great care is needed here. There are analogies with work conducted on broadcast TV news 20–30 years ago. Newsmakers increasingly used entertainment show production techniques to the detriment of news content (Postman, 1985; Gunter, 1987; Robinson and Levy, 1985). These techniques may enhance 'interest' but may actually impede learning and information pay-off.

There is indirect evidence to refute the claim that today's young people do not like being passive recipients of information (Kipnis and Childs, 2005) or that they want to learn through exploration (Windham, 2005). In fact, many research studies show that young scholars have a distinct disinclination to explore. This appears to be a manifestation of a general inclination to take the easiest route possible in undertaking tasks. Shenton and Dixon (2004) for example, found that in researching for school assignments, pupils used the same sources (e.g. same website or book) over a number of searches. Unsurprisingly, these were often the most convenient or accessible sources used (e.g. a reference book at home). Similarly, Fidel et al. (1999) found that students kept exploration to a minimum, even ignoring multimedia in an effort to complete tasks with the least effort possible.

3 The Google Generation has shifted decisively to digital forms of communication, preferring typing to handwriting (e.g. Frand, 2000), messaging to talking on the phone (e.g. Windham, 2005).

It is almost certainly true that many children are acquiring advanced key skills, both for using mobile phones and computer keyboards, but the popularity of messaging is probably determined largely by its low cost relative to voice, so it is difficult to see this as a fundamental trend. Windham's (2005, 56) assertion that today's students eschew the telephone may also only be partially true. She claims that 'it's not that we can't use the telephone . . . it's just that doing so is much more difficult. Using e-mail to set up meetings, ask simple questions, or send in excuses for absences has become so commonplace that few students turn to anything else'. Although not explicitly saying so, it seems clear that the communication here is between student and university staff. By contrast, Agosto and Hughes-Hassell (2005, 154) found that many of their sample of (younger) respondents (aged 14–17) expressed only 'limited interest in communicating via computers (internet, e-mail) [feeling that] (cellular) telephones were more convenient and afforded increased personal contact', albeit the study looked at general information seeking, and did not focus on communication with superiors/staff, etc.

We are not aware of any research that really digs deep into these issues. Anecdotally, it seems likely that many children would prefer to type an assignment rather than use handwriting, but the deeper question raised above cannot be answered at the moment, we think it is still wide open.

4 The Google Generation is impatient and has zero tolerance for delay, information and entertainment needs must be fulfilled immediately. (e.g. Johnson, 2006; Shih and Allen, 2006)

We feel this is a truism of the age in which we live and crosses all generational boundaries in the digital environment, as CIBER deep log studies (Nicholas, Huntington and Watkinson, 2003; Nicholas et al., 2004; Nicholas, Huntington and Watkinson, 2005; Jamali, Nicholas and

Huntington, 2005; Nicholas et al., 2006) have shown time after time. The speed of new media has cultivated a lowered tolerance for delay. Furthermore, the 'anthropomorphization' of technology (Luczak, Roetting and Schmidt, 2003) means that users respond to computerized devices in the way they do to people. People assign personalities to technologies, especially interactive technologies, and expect them to respond in the same way. There is apparently no evidence to suggest that young people are more impatient in this regard than older people. All we can do is to repeat the obvious: that older age groups have memories that pre-date digital media experiences: the younger constituency does not.

5 The Google Generation finds peers more credible as a source of information than authority figures. (e.g. Manuel, 2002)

On balance, we think this is a myth. It depends of course on the specific context: the popularity of social networking does not provide evidence *per se* that immediate peers are valued over authoritative content, merely that technology is being used to cement existing social and collaborative networks, extending them where necessary.

Research in the specific context of the information resources that children prefer and value in a secondary school setting (e.g. Lenhart, Madden and Hitlin, 2005) shows that teachers, relatives and textbooks are consistently valued above the internet for helping to complete homework assignments. We feel that this claim is not incisive: it seems to have more to do with social networking sub-culture and teenagers' naturally rebellious tendencies. Its specific application to the world of education and libraries is pretty questionable.

6 The Google Generation needs to feel constantly connected to the web and to social and family networks. (Frand, 2000)

This may be true of some but not all users. The significance and nature of these connections will vary as a function of the user's personality and background and some will develop a stronger dependence on social networks than others (Lenhart, 2007; Lenhart, Madden and Hitlin, 2005). And older people are catching up fast in terms of their use of online networks:

> 'Lots of people think that older people are not plugged into the digital world. This is clearly wrong,' said an Age Concern spokesman. 'Many are extremely engaged with the internet and use it regularly to keep in touch with family, to shop and take part in communities.'
>
> (*The Daily Telegraph*, 23 August 2007)

We are not aware of any detailed research on this topic, particularly into people's motivations for going online at different stages in their lives: which web services they use, when, why, and how they value the online experience. Recently released data from Ofcom (2007) reveals that the over-65s spend four hours a week *longer* online than 18–24s so, while we may agree with the general sentiment, with exceptions, we are more than a little sceptical that this is a specific 'Google Generation' trait.

7 The Google Generation prefers quick information in the form of easily digested short chunks rather than full text. (e.g. Geck, 2006)

There is overwhelming evidence from CIBER deep log studies of a distinctive form of information behaviour associated with students (e.g. Nicholas and Huntington, 2007a, 2007b). Compared with faculty, they conduct many more sessions but view relatively few pages. They rely on simple thematic (rather than author) searches and are actually less likely than staff to view abstracts rather than full text. However, both students and staff share a general tendency to shallow, horizontal, 'flicking' behaviour in digital libraries. Scanning (described as 'Power browsing' in a recent report [Rowlands and Tenopir, 2007]) and short viewing are the norm for all: reading appears to be only occasionally undertaken online, more often offline or not at all. In the strict sense of a specific Google Generation trait, we think that this claim is not supported. We all do this, and there is no reason to suppose that young people read more when they were required in the past to flick through hard-copy journal volumes.

There is considerable evidence to support the view that many students do not explore information in any deep or reflective manner. The lack of any evaluative efforts on the part of information users has been well documented. According to Levin and Arafeh (2002) most students stop searching at 'good enough' rather than trying to find the best source, etc. Some view the internet as a way to complete their school work as quickly and painlessly as possible, with minimal effort and minimal engagement. For some, of course, this includes viewing the internet as a mechanism for plagiarizing material or otherwise cheating – a practice described by Valenza (2006) as 'slacker culture'.

The information behaviour of young people

The aim of the previous section was to show how very easy it is to invent narratives around the assumed information behaviour of young people. Some things look very different in the internet world, others are much the same and we should beware falling into the trap that behaviour is technologically (rather than socially, cognitively or economically) determined. For this reason, a very close reading of the available evidence is needed.

Use of information and communication technologies

Studies of how young people use information and communication technologies (ICTs), specifically in the form of the internet, in their every-day lives began appearing in the late 1990s. An early researcher (Sjoberg, 1999, 129) found that young people were early adopters of the internet for a variety of tasks, with communication being central: the 'school yard' was no longer the obvious meeting place for young people. A similar observation was made by Pivec (1998), who found that a major youthful use of the internet was for looking for, and choosing, friends. Holloway and Valentine (2001) also found this to be a major feature of computer use in the home.

D'Esposito and Gardner (1999) added that in addition to communicating with and locating friends and relatives, downloading music was a popular internet pastime: a practice that is still popular. By 1997, the computer was the most popular device for listening to music (81%), although only 25% of respondents listened online. A decade later, the popularity of downloads (41%) overtook music purchased in shops (33%) in young people's collections (Synovate, 2007).

It appears that from the beginning of its appearance in the home, the internet has been used for recreational purposes, particularly as a communication medium. Obviously, the technology has moved on and there are now more ways in which these things can be undertaken. The internet is now available on an ever widening array of platforms and devices: it is perhaps, therefore, not surprising that young people use the internet more than television (Synovate, 2007; Los Angeles Times, 2007b). An interesting claim is that the so-called 'Net Generation' is more likely these days to log on to a news website for the latest information than to turn on CNN on the television (Windham, 2005). Of course, the difference here is one of medium, rather than the source itself. The CNN website may well be one consulted in preference to its TV partner – not, therefore, representing much of a radical change. At the time of writing, no peer-reviewed literature has yet reported young people's use of blogs or other personal web space sites in terms of preferred news sources, and the distinction between TV viewing and internet activity is becoming blurred by the presence of TV channels broadcasting entirely or selectively over the internet (one can now watch BBC News 24 on the web, for example, raising the spectre of being in the quantum 'super position' of both watching and not watching TV at the same time).

A common theme in popular discourse is the stereotype of young people as computer whizzes, with a deep knowledge and understanding of hardware and software. This is not borne out by the evidence. It is furthermore dangerous to elide notions of computer and information literacy, a tendency that is very apparent in many representations of the Google Generation. After all, there is a considerable difference between computer and library skills.

Much has been said recently about the apparent expertise of children using electronic resources. Indeed, the prestigious Pew Internet and American Life Project's 'Digital Disconnect' (Levin and Arafeh, 2002, ii and iii) was writing about 'the widening gap between internet-savvy students and their schools' six years ago, claiming from interviews with young people that they use the internet for 'dozens of different education-related uses', including as a 'virtual tutor . . . textbook and reference library . . . guidance counsellor . . . (and) study group', whilst their schools 'have not yet responded to the new ways in which students [use] the Internet'.

On the same theme, Hay (2000, unpaginated) opines that 'Net Generation kids tend to be far more comfortable with and more proficient using information technologies than are their parents or teachers'. More specifically, Baird and Fisher (2005, 12) claim that young people are 'technologically savvy' and 'especially adept at quickly scanning a web page and deciding which links hold the promise of producing a "mother load" of information or valuable content'. This assumption, that levels of digital literacy amongst children of a given age range have risen with ever more exposure to the technology, is prevalent in popular and professional accounts of young people in the internet age (e.g. Kipnis and Childs, 2005; Windham, 2005).

For all the rhetoric, the reality of many young people's use of ICTs is rather more mundane, as recent survey work indicates:

> Virtually 100% of students use word processors and utilize the internet for coursework. But the impression of broad competence slips when percentages are revealed for other applications, such as those for presentation development (65%), spreadsheets (63%), graphics (49%) or creating web pages (25%).
>
> (Oblinger and Hawkins, 2006, 12)

Interestingly, social networking, heralded as the innovation set to 'rapidly chang[e] the face of education' (Baird and Fisher, 2005) 'may not be enjoying the rampant success that has been assumed in the media' (e.g. Walters, 2007). Recent market research has found that 'only a quarter of respondents have ever used social networking sites like MySpace and blogging is still very niche (only 15% ever do it)' (Synovate, 2007, unpaginated). However, a Bloomberg entertainment poll (Los Angeles Times, 2007a) found that half of young adults visit social networking sites, but usage drops away rapidly for those aged over 21. Clearly, as with many other aspects of the adoption of new technology, more research is needed, but the message from our reading of the literature is that it is not helpful to apply broad-brush assumptions about computer whizzery to a whole generation.

Information-searching behaviour

Expertise in formulating search expressions and generally interrogating information systems (predominantly, of course, these days, the internet) has been a preoccupation of researchers for a long time. There is, in fact, little evidence in the literature generated for claims that young people are expert searchers, or even that the search prowess of young people has improved with time. Studies pre-date not only the internet but other electronic systems. Solomon (1993, 247), for example, describes a study by Joyce and Joyce (1970) in which researchers 'implemented a prototype data bank and observed children using its index scheme to find answers that would be sufficient to teach a classmate about a chosen topic'. In a later study, which approximated an electronic environment a little more, Moore and St. George (1991) investigated the information retrieval process used by grade six children (11-year-olds) in New Zealand, in an assignment about birds. Much difficulty was reported in selecting search terms with which to find appropriate material from a card catalogue, and participants did not try alternative terms if their original efforts proved unsuccessful.

In the world of electronic media, Solomon (1993, 259) also found that children had difficulties formulating appropriate terms, due to their 'use of natural language questions ('how to build bird's nests' [sic]); and multiple concepts ('horses poetry' [sic])'. Spavold (1990, 619) found children were 'less confident' in 'problem-solving' database queries when compiling and interrogating a database of family records, and that their grasp of commands was 'confused and easily forgotten'. With adequate support and training, however, participants in both of these early studies were able to acquire a basic level of competence.

Later, Hirsh (1999) found that students considered only the presence or absence of words exactly describing their search topic/matching their search terms in deciding relevance. By focusing so narrowly on this aspect of material retrieved, they missed many other relevant documents. He also found that students did not use advanced search facilities or navigation aids.

Chen (2003) also noted difficulties in formulating search queries, claiming that 'children and youth' have trouble generating alternative search terms/synonyms (when the original terms prove fruitless) and often repeat the same search several times. Not surprisingly, they also encountered great difficulties in narrowing a search. Also unsurprisingly, the literature consistently suggests that students do not plan searches in advance (Bilal, 2001; Large et al., 1998; Shenton and Dixon, 2004).

One manifestation of the lack of query formulation is the prevalence of full phrase searching by young people (as noted above, by Solomon, 1993). A review by Schacter, Chung and Dorr (1998, 847), for example, of the search logs associated with children's (given) search tasks, indicated that 20 of the 32 children used full sentence requests, such as, 'What are the three most common crimes in California?' and 'How to reduce crime in California?' in their query formulations. Other researchers (e.g. Chen, 2003; Bilal, 2000) have also noted young people's propensity for full phrase searching.

It would be tempting to attribute the prevalence of full-phrase search strings with the rise in the accessibility of the internet: the web, of course, provides extensive support for natural language searching. This is taken to its logical conclusion in 'Ask.com' (previously 'Ask Jeeves') which encourages users to enter full phrases as search terms (the help section includes this advice: 'the following search example should successfully lead you to the desired information: "where can I find cheap airfares to New York?"') (Ask.com, 2007, unpaginated). However, a scrutiny of the literature shows that the practice of formulating queries in this way pre-dates the web. Marchionini (1989, 61) is one researcher who noted such queries on a CD-ROM encyclopedia. Younger subjects ['3rd and 4th graders', or 8 and 9 year olds] 'were more likely to use actual sentences to query the system' although many older participants (10–11 year olds) also adopted this practice. From her review of the literature Valenza concludes that students assume search

engines 'understand' sentences and questions (Valenza, 2006). With regard
to young people's understanding of the way information is organized, the
way results are returned, and differences in search interfaces, Valenza sums
up previous literature nicely in saying that many youngsters only have a
'limited understanding' of these aspects of ICT use (citing Fidel et al., 1999;
Bilal and Kirby, 2002; Chen, 2003).

The ubiquitous use of search engines defines a conceptual model for
information retrieval (IR) at an early age. The translation of this model into
traditional retrieval systems, such as library catalogues and bibliographic
databases, or federated search tools such as MetaLib, which provide
controlled access to organized information, may be problematic and has
implications for future user awareness and training programmes (Brophy and
Bawden, 2005). Muramatsu and Pratt (2001) report that users have
difficulty in understanding how search engines transform queries by using a
variety of default search mechanisms, such as automatic Boolean operators,
stop words, truncation and term order sensitivity. Thus cognitive models of
the internet, domain knowledge and understanding of the terminology,
spelling, grammar and sentence structure contribute to the inability,
particularly amongst younger children (under 13 years) and older users
(46–64) to construct effective searches and evaluate the results (Slone, 2003).

> Students usually approach their research without regard to the library's
> structure or the way that library segments different resources into different
> areas of its web site. Library web sites often reflect an organizational view of
> the library . . . they do not do a particularly good job of aggregating content
> on a particular subject area.
>
> (Oblinger and Hawkins, 2006, 12)

Access to, and familiarity with, the internet may also impact on the Google
Generation's information-seeking skills and their educational aspirations.
Factors such as policies and rules, technological and filtering controls and
time constraints on teachers' ability to support the development of
information literacy within the curriculum, restrict access to the internet in
schools and prevent students from maximizing the potential of the internet

in educational activities (Selwyn, 2006; Williams and Wavell, 2006).

Recent reports identify generational differences as obstacles to inform-ation-seeking behaviour (Lorenzo, Oblinger and Dziuban, 2006; Lorenzo and Dziuban, 2006; Jones, 2002; Levin and Arafeh, 2002) and forecast challenges for information provision in higher education. The potential for misunderstandings and communication problems, derived from linguistic incompatibilities between digital natives and digital immigrants who use different languages to describe technology-related activities according to their experience and degree of immersion in the digital world and level of information savviness, will increase (Oblinger 2003). The findings of these studies raise some real questions about the ability of schools and colleges to develop the search capabilities of the Google Generation to a level appropriate to the demands of higher education and research. Indeed, there appears to be a marked lack of support by teachers and other carers when it comes to information retrieval, possibly due – ironically – to the perceived ease with which digital systems (as exemplified by the web) can be searched. A com-mon theme of several studies (e.g. Bilal and Kirby, 2002; Hirsh, 1999; Fidel et al., 1999; Oblinger and Hawkins, 2006) is that more training is needed to enable school children to make really effective use of digital technologies.

Such training need not be generic. The need for targeted instructional activities, which recognize disciplinary differences in information-seeking behaviour, and the specific needs of remote, off-campus users have been identified by Whitmire (2001). Gardner and Eng (2005) consider the implications for academic libraries of differences in the learning styles of Net Generation students, who have high expectations of IT infrastructures and round-the-clock access. Group work, peer learning, electronic learning environments such as BlackBoard and Moodle, and remote access to information resources for distance learning, contribute to a need to support:

- demand for quality academic facilities and high academic achievement
- the need for customization of technology and research
- the need for integration of technology into learning
- the usage of new communication modes.

Initiatives designed to support users outside the physical library, for example the 'Roving Librarian' project at Harvard that, in spring 2003, placed librarians equipped with wireless-enabled laptops in spaces such as the students union, are quoted in Gardner and Eng (2005). Other innovative tactics such as relentless promotion, instruction and customer service are recommended to overcome barriers and market the support that users seem to consider unnecessary.

Information evaluation skills

One aspect of youthful information behaviour, one of great concern, is the way that young people evaluate, or rather fail to evaluate, information from electronic sources. Again, there is little evidence that this behavioural trait has changed over the last 10 or 15 years. Two main issues dominate the literature: relevance and quality/authority. With regard to the first of these, relevance, Chen (1993) was suggesting 15 years ago that teenagers do not review the information they retrieve (in this case from an online database) and, consequently, they undertake unnecessary and wasteful supplementary searches. Later Schacter et al. (1998) found that the speed of young people's web searching also indicated that little time could possibly be spent in evaluating information (a finding echoed by Chen, 2003). In another study from the late 1990s, Williams (1999) observed juvenile information-seeking stopping at the point where articles were found and printed, especially with regard to younger users. Little regard was made to the text itself – a word in the title, or an appropriate accompanying image was enough to confirm relevance. Maintaining this trend into the 2000s, Merchant and Hepworth (2002, 84) studied the research habits of 40 pupils aged 10-16 years, and found that teachers complained that, when their charges found articles using difficult language, 'they just print off or copy down and hand in'. Hsieh-Yee (2001) reviewing literature on internet use generally, also concluded, from a résumé of papers on children's usage behaviour, that they experience great difficulty judging the quality of web pages.

Researchers have similarly found a lack of attention young people give to the issue of authority. Hirsh (1999), for example, found that students did not consider at all issues of authority of source when evaluating websites. Grimes and Boening (2001, 19, 20) relate that in a case study of 50 'freshmen' students in the USA, participants evaluated web resources in terms of quality of information 'only superficially, if at all'. In fact, they were 'ill-equipped and unwilling to evaluate resources'. Lorenzen (2001) found in his interviews with 15–17-year-olds, that many thought that if a site was indexed by Yahoo it had to be authoritative, and so the question of evaluating websites naturally did not arise. A later study, by Shenton and Dixon (2003c), found that there was no attempt by anyone, in any of the age groups studied (in the range 4–16), to verify information, and evaluative skills were lacking. Merchant and Hepworth (2002, 85) suggested that it was 'difficult for students to understand that the first solution they find may not be the only answer'.

D'Esposito and Gardner (1999), however, claim that in a qualitative study of 14 mainly undergraduates (admittedly, older than the school-aged children studied by Shenton and Dixon), participants used many criteria for evaluating the quality of website and the reliability of the information: 'authorship or page ownership, links to other sites, and the possibility of validation from other sources' (D'Esposito and Gardner 1999, 458). However, in this study, participants were asked what steps they undertook to evaluate material, thus possibly introducing a Hawthorne effect. Studies such as that by Shenton and Dixon (2003c) – in which participants were observed rather than prompted – or those such as by Schacter, Chung, and Dorr (1998) – where participants are asked simply to rate information consistently – find that evaluative skills are barely in evidence.

Many reports on internet use, particularly those published by bodies such as EDUCAUSE, identify trends that cannot be ignored by the academic community, such as the imminent influx of 'internet savvy' students, to whom resources like Google and Wikipedia, and instant messaging and social networking environments such as Facebook and MySpace, are second nature, into an environment populated by aging faculty (Oblinger, 2003). Members of the 'born-digital' Google Generation apparently bring with them a confidence in using the internet for information retrieval purposes which belies their skills in critical evaluation and devising search strategies (Lorenzo and Dziuban, 2006; Rogers and Swan, 2004).

Young people's use of libraries

Regarding their use, understanding and awareness of library services, the research literature indicates that even in the early 2000s, large numbers of young people are unaware that libraries offer internet access. A recent study by Corradini (2006, 490), for example, found that only 42% of youngsters knew this, despite being library users. Indeed, the image of the library was still 'almost completely bound to its traditional printed materials'. The Online Computer Library Center (OCLC, 2002) found that although 70% of university students used their library websites for some assignment-related information, only 20% did so for *most* assignments. Full-text articles are used the most often (67%), with e-books (21%) and online reference (6%) being used the least often. However, a full 90% of students also use their library's print resources, again reinforcing the view that the library is still seen as predominantly print based by many young people. A contrasting UK survey (Myhill, 2007) found that the library OPAC and university web pages were well used, especially by students in their final year, but this may well have been influenced by the study design, which comprised an online questionnaire hosted on the library website.

Findings indicating a lack of appreciation of the premium electronic content provided by libraries reflect those of earlier studies, and appear to indicate little change in terms of young people's perception of libraries. For example, in D'Esposito and Gardner's (1999, 458) study of undergraduates' views on libraries and the internet, although participants acknowledged that the internet was available in the library and that library web pages existed, 'the general perception was that the library and the Internet were two separate and unrelated entities'.

Early studies also corroborate later work with regard to the perceptions of 'libraries' and 'the Internet'. Fidel et al. (1999) found that for his small sample of 11th and 12th grade students (17 and 18 year olds) a visit to the school library was both time consuming and labour intensive. Study participants all preferred to research information independently on the internet. This attitude appears to persist. Pavey (2006) claimed, from personal experience, that children often arrive at higher education level never having used a library. Even where the library is acknowledged to have a variety of electronic resources, these may not be well exploited. In an opinion piece, Lippincott (2005) claimed that students often found 'library-sponsored' sources of information difficult to negotiate, and so preferred to use the more simplistic solutions offered by Google.

Young people and the social web

The emergence of social websites is changing the nature and fabric of the world wide web: we have moved from an internet built by a few thousand authors to one being constructed in real time by millions. Social networking is of particular interest to librarians and publishers because it is part of a wider trend: users creating and posting content for themselves, thus blurring the age-old distinction between information producers and information consumers. And as desktop publishing software becomes the norm, it is sometimes almost impossible to tell the difference between formally published and self-published material.

This is a phenomenon affecting the whole of society and the current popularity of social networking among the young perhaps diverts attention from who actually generates (as opposed to who consumes) user-generated content: Wikipedia and YouTube both exhibit a marked age separation between viewers of content (mainly 18–24-year-olds) and content generators (mainly 45–54-year-olds and 35–44-year-olds respectively) (Horrigan, 2007).

Many librarians have started to experiment with social software in an attempt to get closer to their users. They have a problem. Although research libraries spend millions of pounds providing seamless desktop access to expensive copyrighted electronic content – journals, books and monographs – much of this is news to their users. Either they do not know that the library provides this material, or they get to it, possibly via Google, and assume it is 'free'. Libraries are increasingly between a rock and a hard place:

the publisher or search engine gets the credit, they just pick up the tab.

So, a number of 'progressive' librarians have started building a presence in MySpace and Facebook by creating institutional profiles. It is too early for a solid evidence base to emerge to see whether this kind of initiative will bear fruit, but there are clearly dangers in trying to appear 'cool' to a younger audience. In fact, there is a considerable danger that younger users will resent the library invading what they may regard as their space (as, indeed, the very choice of label 'MySpace' implies). There is a big difference between 'being where our users are' and 'being USEFUL to our users where they are' (OCLC, 2007).

This seems to be the message from a recent OCLC survey in which college students and members of the general public were asked the following question: How likely would you be to participate in each of the following activities on a social networking or community site if built by your library?:

- self-publish creative work: 7% (6%)
- share ideas about library services: 10% (7%)
- share your photos/videos: 7% (6%)
- participate in online discussion groups: 6% (6%)
- meet others with similar interests: 6% (7%)
- describe your own personal collections: 9% (6%)
- view others' personal collections: 12% (6%).

The percentages given are those who say they are *extremely likely* or *very likely* to do so (general public responses in brackets).

Thus, most college students say they are not interested (OCLC, 2007). Clearly it is very early days, but these survey findings do not provide much confidence that social software, yet, has much to contribute to the rebuilding of relationships with users in an increasingly disintermediated environment.

There are many other examples of library experimentation with Web 2.0 technologies – for example to enrich catalogue entries with user reviews and ratings – but it is again simply too early to assess their impact or effectiveness. But there is no doubting that social networking is a major success story and that libraries should be keeping a watching brief over developments in this area, especially as there is evidence from the US that most students with online access use social networking technologies at least sometimes and that many report using these networks to discuss education-related topics (OCLC, 2007).

What do we really know about young people's information behaviour?

Research into how children and young people become competent in using the internet and other research tools is patchy but some consistent themes are beginning to emerge:

- The information literacy of young people has not improved with the widening access to technology: in fact, their apparent facility with computers disguises some worrying problems.
- Internet research shows that the speed of young people's web searching means that little time is spent in evaluating information, either for relevance, accuracy or authority.
- Young people have a poor understanding of their information needs and thus find it difficult to develop effective search strategies.
- As a result, they exhibit a strong preference for expressing themselves in natural language rather than analysing which key words might be more effective.
- Faced with a long list of search hits, young people find it difficult to assess the relevance of the materials presented and often print off pages with no more than a perfunctory glance at them (to be fair, the information tasks that they are often set in school are no more than treasure hunts where finding information is an end in itself).
- Use of the physical library is in decline.

These points relate both to the current use of the internet by young people and, a technology generation earlier, to their use of early online systems and CD-ROMs. There is no real direct evidence that young people's information literacy is any better or worse than before. However, the ubiquitous use of highly-branded search engines raises other issues:

- Young people have unsophisticated mental maps of what the internet is, often failing to appreciate that it is a collection of networked resources from different providers.
- As a result, the search engine, be that Yahoo or Google, becomes the primary brand that they associate with the internet.
- Many young people do not find library-sponsored resources intuitive and therefore prefer to use Google or Yahoo instead: these offer a familiar, if simplistic, solution for their study needs.

The huge question raised above is whether, and to what extent, the behaviour, attitudes and preferences of today's Google Generation youngsters will persist as they grow up and some of them become academics and scholars. In the absence of properly constructed longitudinal studies that track the information behaviour of a single cohort of young people through to maturity, it is impossible to answer this question directly. People have different information needs at different points in their lives. There are very very few controlled studies that account for age and information-seeking behaviour systematically: as a result there is much mis-information and much speculation about how young people supposedly behave in cyberspace.

Work by Nicholas and Huntington (2007a, 2007b) has addressed this issue directly by investigating the behaviour of a wide range of ages on the same content platforms: BL Learning, a service aimed at schoolchildren and teachers, and Intute, a JISC service that is aimed across the whole university community.

The key points to emerge from this experiment are:

- Both services are very popular, especially with Americans, and attract a great deal of use (in the case of BL Learning, 14% of all British Library traffic) strongly suggesting that they contain content that younger scholars (and their teachers) value highly.
- The popularity of both sites suggests they have significant brand presence at home and abroad.
- For both sites, the majority of visits were traffic directed from a search engine, and they were interrogated from home, rather than from school or college.
- About 40% of school search engine users found BL Learning using an image search, suggesting a preference for this kind of retrieval.
- Those entering BL Learning via a blog type link were in a very small minority and these were predominantly North Americans (and core site users), no evidence yet that social networking has really caught on in the context of library sites.
- However, not all use appears to be very productive and both sites exhibited high levels of bouncing activity, probably due to mis-directed Google traffic.

Young scholars are using tools that require little skill: they appear satisfied with a very simple or basic form of searching. Thus, in the case of Intute, it was found that the more pages viewed in a session, the greater the likelihood that that session clicked through to another site (an outcome in the case of a 'gateway' site like Intute).

Findings from CIBER's deep log analysis work are very consistent with the information seeking literature and other research based on observations or surveys. For example, observational studies have shown that young people scan online pages very rapidly (boys especially) and click extensively on hyperlinks – rather than reading sequentially. Users make very little use of advanced search facilities, assuming that search engines 'understand' their queries. They tend to move rapidly from page to page, spending little time reading or digesting information and they have difficulty making relevance judgments about the pages they retrieve. As outlined above, the literature also shows that many of these characteristics pre-date the web, and so they cannot be projected on to the internet as something completely new.

Thus, there is very little evidence of generational shifts in the literature to support the view that today's Google Generation youngsters are fundamentally 'different' from previous cohorts. This is, of course, difficult to interpret: there are no longitudinal studies providing robust evidence to refute or confirm this. On balance, the literature appears to point to a big distinction between young children and teenage groups, probably due to the fact that small children have not yet developed the cognitive and motor skills to be effective searchers. Beyond age 11, the message is continuity. Children do not seem especially different in their behaviour from young adults.

So, in a sense, we are all Google Generation now: the demographics of internet and media consumption are rapidly eroding this presumed generational difference. Surveys tell us that older internet users, or digital immigrants, quickly develop skills to a similar level of expertise. Many baby boomers and those over 65 are engaging in online activity, often to communicate with family members. Experience with digital technology at work means that 50–64 year olds use the internet as much as other groups and over 65s spend 42 hours a month on the internet, compared with teenagers' 25 hours (Lenhart, Simon and Graziano, 2001; Ofcom, 2006). Such evidence indicates that more people across all age groups are using the internet and Web 2.0 technologies widely and for a variety of purposes. The young (not just the Google Generation but also Generation Y, the next one up) may have been the earliest adopters but now older users are fast catching up . . . the so-called Silver Surfers. In many ways the Google Generation label is increasingly unhelpful. Recent research finds that it is not even accurate within the cohort of young people that it seeks to stereotype. For example, recent consumer market research finds that only 27% of UK teenagers could really be described as having the kind of deep interest and facility in IT that the label implies. The majority ('average Joes', 57%) use relatively low-level technology to support their basic communication or entertainment needs and there is a substantial residuum of 20% ('digital dissidents') who actively dislike technology and avoid using it wherever possible (Synovate, 2007). The demographics are clearly very complicated and resistant to neat generational labelling. Much of the evidence gained from a recent re-analysis of earlier work by Carol Tenopir and Don King (Rowlands and Tenopir, 2007) suggests that the differences in information behaviour, at a single point in time, between young and early middle-aged students, are much less significant than those between young and more mature (40- and 50-year-old) students.

Whether or not our young people really have lower levels of traditional information skills than before, we are simply not in a position to know. However, the stakes are much higher now in an educational setting where 'self-directed learning' is the norm. An interim conclusion, therefore, from the increasing body of research literature, is that much writing on the topic of young people's information skills overestimates the impact of ICTs on the young and underestimates its effect on older generations. A much greater sense of balance is needed.

The information literacy agenda

All this discussion is, of course, of great relevance to the world of education, especially given the emphasis, at school and at university, on coursework and other forms of self-directed learning.

Yet there is very little systematic research in the UK into the information skills of young people in, and entering, higher education. This is symptomatic of a lack of strategic government support for information literacy programmes and we should all be concerned about this:

> The most significant finding [of our study] was that, although the teachers interviewed were information literate, their skills with and attitudes towards information literacy were not being transferred to their pupils.
>
> (Merchant and Hepworth, 2002)

A much fuller research picture is available in the USA, however, and it paints a picture of a large minority of freshmen entering college and university with low levels of information literacy and high levels of library anxiety. As might be expected, information skills correlate positively with entry-level SAT scores and subsequent grades (Gross and Latham, 2007).

It is not reasonable to translate these findings into the UK context but, since information literacy training is so patchy and inconsistent in this country, the US experience is worth noting. There are two particularly powerful messages emerging from recent research (Gross and Latham, 2007). When the top and bottom quartiles of students – as defined by their information literacy skills – are compared, it emerges that the top quartile report a much higher incidence of exposure to basic library skills from their parents, in the school library, classroom or public library in their earlier years. It seems that a new divide is opening up in the US, with the better-equipped students taking the prizes of better grades. At the lower end of the information skills spectrum, the research finds that intervention at university age is too late: these students have already developed an ingrained coping behaviour, they have learned to 'get by' with Google and, presumably, not even to consider it as 'getting by' but being expert (Gross and Latham, 2007). The problem here is that they simply do not recognize that they have a problem. There is a big gap between their actual performance in information literacy tests and their self-estimates of information skill and library anxiety. The findings of these studies raise questions about the ability of schools and colleges to develop the search capabilities of the Google Generation to a level appropriate to the demands of higher education and research. In addition, a recent survey in this country (the UK) by the Association of Teachers and Lecturers (ATL, 2008) identifies plagiarism as a major problem amongst sixth-form pupils because of the ease with which information can be cut and pasted into coursework, with little regard for real meaning or understanding. This raises the concern that their ability to cope with higher level work is under threat.

Information skills need to be developed during formative school years – remedial information literacy programmes at university level are likely to be ineffective, at least so says the US experience.

Policy implications

The library community needs to invest more in data collection and analysis and to take its examples from commercial leaders (for example, Tesco) which have a much more detailed and insightful understanding of their customer base and preferences. In particular, there is a need for ongoing longitudinal data and intelligence functions to provide a vital early radar warning of oncoming change. It would be useful for major national libraries to have in-house user studies departments. Without this intelligence, service stereotypes can easily become detached from reality.

At national level, there is a desperate need for a well-funded programme of educational research and inquiry into the information and digital literacy skills of our young people. If the erratic behaviour we are seeing in digital libraries really is the result of failure at the library terminal, then society has a major problem. Information skills are needed more than ever and at a higher level if people are to really avail themselves of the benefits of an information society.

Emerging research findings from the US point to the fact that these skills need to be inculcated during the formative years of childhood: by university or college it is too late to reverse engineer deeply ingrained habits, notably an uncritical trust in branded search engines to deliver quick fixes.

This will require concerted action between libraries, schools and parents.

References

Agosto, D. E. (2002) A Model of Young People's Decision-Making in Using the Web, *Library and Information Science Research*, **24** (4), 311–41.

Agosto, D. E. (2006) Toward a Model of the Everyday Life Information Needs of Urban Teenagers, Part 1: theoretical model, *Journal of the American Society for Information Science and Technology*, **57** (10), 1394–1403.

Agosto, D. E. and Hughes-Hassell, S. (2005) People, Places and Questions: an investigation of the everyday life information-seeking behaviors of urban young adults, *Library and Information Science Research*, **27**, 141–63.

Ask.com (2007) Ask.com Search Tips, Ask.com website, http://sp.uk/ask.com/en/docs/about/tipsforsearching.shtml [accessed 18 July 2007].

ATL (2008) *School Work Plagued by Plagiarism,* www.atl.org.uk.

Baird, D. and Fisher, M. (2005) Neomillenial User Experience Design Strategies: utilizing social networking media to support 'always on' learning styles, *Journal of Educational Technology Systems*, **34** (1), 5–32.

BBC Online (2005) Worksheet: Half-Blood Prince Sets UK Record, *CBBC News* website,
http://news.bbc.co.uk/bbcnews/hi/newsid_4700000/newsid_4701400/4701409.stm [accessed 18 July 2007].

Bilal, D. (2000) Children's Use of the Yahooligans! Web Search Engine: I. cognitive, physical, and affective behaviors on fact-based tasks, *Journal of the American Society for Information Science*, **51** (7), 646–65.

Bilal, D. (2001) Children's Use of the Yahooligans! Web Search Engine: II. cognitive and physical behaviors on research tasks, *Journal of the American Society for Information Science and Technology*, **52** (2), 118–36.

Bilal, D. (2002) Perspectives on Children's Navigation of the World Wide Web: does the type of search task make a difference?, *Online Information Review*, **26** (2), 108–17.

Bilal, D. and Kirby, J. (2002) Differences and Similarities in Information Seeking: children and adults as web users, *Information Processing and Management*, **38** (5), 649–70.

Borgman, C., Hirsh, S., Walter, V. and Gallagher, A. (1995) Children's Searching Behavior on Browsing and Keyword Online Catalogs: The Science Library Catalog Project, *Journal of the American Society for Information Science*, **46** (9), 663–84.

Brophy, J. and Bawden, D. (2005) Is Google Enough? Comparison of an internet search engine with academic library resources, *Aslib Proceedings*, **57** (6), 498–512.

Chen, S. (1993) A Study of High School Students' Online Catalog Searching Behavior, *School Library Media Quarterly*, **22** (1), 33–40.

Chen, S. (2003) Searching the Online Catalog and Web, *Journal of Educational Media and Library Sciences*, **41** (1), 29-43.

Clarke, A. and Foster, A. (2005) *Children's and Young People's Reading Habits and Preferences: the who, what, why, where and when*, National Literacy Trust.

Corradini, E. (2006) Teenagers Analyse their Public Library, *New Library World*, **107** (1230/1231), 481–98.

D'Esposito, J. and Gardner, R. (1999) University Students' Perceptions of the Internet: an exploratory study, *The Journal of Academic Librarianship*, **25** (6), 456–61.

Fidel, R., Davies, R., Douglas, M., Holder, J., Hopkins, C., Kushner, E., Miyagishima, B. and Toney, C. (1999) A Visit to the Information Mall: web searching behavior of high school students, *Journal of the American Society for Information Science*, **50** (1), 24–37.

Frand, J. L. (2000) Information-Age Mindset: changes in students and implications for higher education, *Educause Review*, **35** (5), 15–24, http://educause.edu.apps/er/erm00/articles005/erm0051.pdf.

Gardner, S. and Eng, S. (2005) What Students Want: Generation Y and the changing function of the academic library, *Libraries and the Academy*, **5** (3), 405–20.

Geck, C. (2006) The Generation Z Connection: teaching information literacy to the newest net generation, *Teacher Librarian*, **33** (3), 19–23.

Grimes, D. and Boening, C. (2001) Worries With the Web: a look at student use of web resources, *College and Research Libraries*, **62** (1), 11–22.

Gross, M. and Latham, D. (2007) Attaining Information Literacy: an investigation of the relationship between skill level, self-estimates of skill, and library anxiety, *Library and Information Science Research*, **29** (3), 332–53.

Gunter, B. (1987) *Poor Reception: misunderstanding and forgetting broadcast news*, Lawrence Erlbaum.

Hay, L. (2000) Educating the Net Generation, *The School Administrator*, www.aasa.org/publications/saarticledetail.cfm?mnitemnumber=.

Haycock, K. and Huang, S. (2001) Are Today's High School Graduates Ready?, *Thinking K-16*, **5** (1), 3–17.

Hirsh, S. G. (1999) Children's Relevance Criteria and Information Seeking on Electronic Resources, *Journal of the American Society for Information Science*, **50** (14), 1265–83.

Holloway, S. and Valentine, G. (2001) Children at Home in the Wired World, *Urban Geography*, **22** (6), 562–83.

Horrigan, J. (2007) *A Typology of Information and Communication Technology Users*, Pew Internet and American Life Project.

Hsieh-Yee, I. (2001) Research on Web Search Behaviour, *Library and Information Science Research*, **23**, 167–85.

Jamali, H. R., Nicholas, D. and Huntington, P. (2005) The Use and Users of Scholarly E-Journals: a review of log analysis studies, *Aslib Proceedings*, **57** (6), 554–71.

Johnson, L. (2006) The Sea Change Before Us, *Educause Review*, March/April, 72–3.

Jones, S. (2002) *The Internet Goes to College*, Pew Internet and American Life Project.

Joyce, B. R. and Joyce, E. A. (1970) The Creation of Information Systems for Children, *Interchange*, **1** (1), 1–12.

Kipnis, D. and Childs, G. (2005) *Educating Generation X and Generation Y: Teaching Tips for Librarians*, Philadelphia PA, Academic and Instructional Support and Resources (AISR) Staff Paper.

Large, A. (2005) Children, Teenagers, and the Web, *Annual Review of Information Science and Technology*, **39** (1), 347–92.

Large, A., Beheshti, J. and Breuleux, A. (1998) Information Seeking in a Multimedia Environment by Primary School Students, *Library and Information Science Research*, **20** (4), 343–76.

Lenhart, A. (2007) *Social Networking Websites and Teens: an overview*, Pew Internet and American Life Project.

Lenhart, A., Madden, M. and Hitlin, P. (2005) *Teens and Technology*, Pew Internet and American Life Project.

Lenhart, A., Simon, M. and Graziano, M. (2001) The Internet and Education: findings of the Pew Internet and American Life Project, www.pewinternet.org.pdfs/PIP_Schools_Report.pdf.

Levin, D. and Arafeh, S. (2002) *The Digital Disconnect: the widening gap between internet-savvy students and their schools*, Pew Internet and American Life Project.

Lippincott, J. (2005) Net Generation Students and Libraries, *Educause Review*, March/April, 56–66.

Loh, C. S. and Williams, M. D. (2002) What's in a Web Site? Student perceptions, *Journal of Research on Technology in Education*, **34** (3), 351–63.

Long, S. (2005) Digital Natives: if you aren't one, get to know one, *New Library World*, **106** (1210/1211), 187–9.

Lorenzen, M. (2001) The Land of Confusion? High school students and their use of the World Wide Web for research, *Research Strategies*, **18** (2), 151–63.

Lorenzo, G. and Dziuban, C. (2006) *Ensuring the Net Generation is Net Savvy* (ELI Paper 2), www.educause.edu/ir/library/pdf/ELI3006.pdf.

Lorenzo, G., Oblinger, D. and Dziuban, C. (2006) *How Choice, Co-Creation and Culture are Changing: What it means to be Net Savvy* (ELI Paper 4), www.educause.edu/ir/library/pdf/ELI3008.pdf.

Los Angeles Times (2007a) *Bloomberg Survey of Pop Culture and Entertainment in the United States: computers, cell phones and multi-tasking,* www.latimes.com/news/custom/timespoll/.

Los Angeles Times (2007b) *Bloomberg Survey of Pop Culture and Entertainment in the United States: Jon Stewart? No Way. Teens Stay Caught Up By Watching Local News,* www.latimes.com/news/custom/timespoll/.

Luczak, H., Roetting, M. and Schmidt, L. (2003) Let's Talk: anthropomorphization as means to cope with stress of interacting with technical devices, *Ergonomics*, **46** (13–14), 1361–74.

McLuhan, M. (1962) *The Gutenberg Galaxy: the making of typographic man,* University of Toronto Press.

Manuel, K. (2002) Teaching Information Literacy to Generation Y, *Journal of Library Administration*, **36**, 195–217.

Marchionini, G. (1989) Information-Seeking Strategies of Novices Using Full-Text Electronic Encyclopedia, *Journal of the American Society for Information Science*, **40** (1), 54–66.

Merchant, L. and Hepworth, M. (2002) Information Literacy of Teachers and Pupils in Secondary Schools, *Journal of Librarianship and Information Science*, **34** (2), 81–9.

Moore, P. and St. George, A. (1991) Children as Information Seekers: the cognitive demands of books and library systems, *School Library Media Quarterly*, **19** (3), 161–8.

Muramatsu, J. and Pratt, W. (2001) Transparent Queries: investigating users' mental models of search engines, *Proceedings of the 24th Annual International ACM SIGIR Conference on Research and Development in Information Retrieval,* New Orleans, Louisiana, 217–24.

Myhill, M. (2007) Canute Rules the Waves? Hope for e-library tools facing the challenge of the 'Google generation', *Program*, **41** (1), 5–19.

Nicholas, D. and Huntington, P. (2007a) *An Evaluation of BL Learning: a web site for younger scholars,* CIBER, University College London, www.ucl.ac.uk/slais/research/ciber/downloads/.

Nicholas, D. and Huntington, P. (2007b) *A User Evaluation of Intute,* CIBER, University College London, www.ucl.ac.uk/slais/research/ciber/downloads/.

Nicholas, D., Huntington, P., Jamali, H. R. and Watkinson, A. (2006) The

Information Seeking Behaviour of the Users of Digital Scholarly Journals, *Information Processing and Management*, **42** (5), 1345–65.

Nicholas, D., Huntington, P. and Watkinson, A. (2003) Digital Journals, Big Deals and Online Searching Behaviour: a pilot study, *Aslib Proceedings*, **55** (1/2), 84–109.

Nicholas, D., Huntington, P. and Watkinson, A. (2005) Scholarly Journal Usage: the results of deep log analysis, *Journal of Documentation*, **61** (2), 248–80.

Nicholas, D., Huntington, P., Williams, P. and Dobrowolski, T. (2004) Re-appraising Information Seeking Behaviour in a Digital Environment: bouncers, checkers, returnees and the like, *Journal of Documentation*, **60** (1), 24–43.

NIFL (2007) *National Assessment of Educational Progress*, National Institute for Literacy, www.nifl.gov/nifl/facts/NAEP.html.

Oblinger, D. (2003) Boomers, Gen-Xers and Millenials: understanding the new students, *Educause Review*, **38** (7), 37–47.

Oblinger, D. and Hawkins, B. (2006) The Myth about Students: IT myths, *Educause Review*, **41** (2), 12–13.

OCLC (2002) *How Academic Librarians Can Influence Students' Web-Based Information Choices*. White Paper on the Information Habits of College Students, Online Computer Library Center.

OCLC (2007) *Sharing, Privacy and Trust in Our Networked World*, Dublin: Computer Library Center.

Ofcom (2006) *The Consumer Experience*, Office for Communications.

Ofcom (2007) *Communications Market Report: converging communications markets. Research Document*, Office for Communications.

Pavey, S. (2006) School Librarians and the Google Generation, *ALISS Quarterly*, **2** (1), 3–7.

Pivec, F. (1998) Surfing Through the Internet: the new content of teenagers' spare time, *Aslib Proceedings*, **50** (4), 88–92.

Postman, N. (1985) *Amusing Ourselves to Death: public discourse in the age of show business*, Penguin.

Prensky, M. (2001) *Digital Natives, Digital Immigrants*, www.marcprensky.com.

Robinson, J. and Levy, M. (1985) *The Main Source: learning from television news*, Sage.

Rodgers, L. (2007) *UK Still Loves a Good Page-Turner*, (BBC News), http://news.bbc.co.uk/1/hi/uk/6287344.stm.

Rogers, D. and Swan, K. (2004) Self-Regulated Learning and the Internet, *Teachers College Record*, **106** (9), 1804–24.

Rowlands, I. and Tenopir, C. (2007) *Age-Related Information Behaviour*, CIBER, University College London, www.ucl.ac.uk/slais/research/ciber/downloads/.

Schacter, J., Chung, G. and Dorr, A. (1998) Children's Internet Searching on Complex Problems: performance and process analyses, *Journal of the American Society for Information Science*, **49** (9), 840–50.

Selwyn, N. (2006) Exploring the 'Digital Disconnect' Between Net-Savvy Students and their Schools, *Learning Media and Technology*, **31** (1), 5–17.

Shenton, A. and Dixon, P. (2003a) A Comparison of Youngsters' Use of CD-ROM and Internet as Information Resources, *Journal of the American Society for Information Science and Technology*, **54** (11), 1029–49.

Shenton, A. and Dixon, P. (2003b) Sequential or Selective Access? Young people's strategies for finding information in non-fiction books, *New Review of Children's Literature and Librarianship*, **9** (1), 57–69.

Shenton, A. and Dixon, P. (2003c) Models of Young People's Information Seeking, *Journal of Librarianship and Information Science*, **35** (1), 5–22.

Shenton, A. and Dixon, P. (2004) Issues Arising from Youngsters' Information-Seeking Behaviour, *Library and Information Science Research*, **26** (2), 177–200.

Shih, W. and Allen, M. (2006) Working with Generation D: adopting and adapting to cultural learning and change, *Library Management*, **28** (1/2), 89–100.

Sjoberg, U. (1999) The Rise of the Electronic Individual: a study of how young Swedish teenagers use and perceive internet, *Telematics and Informatics*, **16** (3), 113–33.

Slone, D. J. (2003) Internet Search Approaches: the influence of age, search goals, and experience, *Library and Information Science Research*, **25** (4), 403–18.

Solomon, P. (1993) Children's Information Retrieval Behaviour: a case study of an OPAC, *Journal of the American Society for Information Science*, **44** (5), 245–64.

Spavold, J. (1990) The Child as Naïve User: a study of database use with young children, *Journal of Man-Machine Studies*, **32** (6), 603–25.

Sullivan, K. (2005) Collection Development for the "Chip" Generation and Beyond, *Collection Building*, **24** (2), 56–60.

Synovate (2007) *Leisure Time: clean living youth shun new technology*, www.synovate.com/current/news/article/2007/02/leisure-time-clean-living-youth-shun-new-technology.html.

Valenza, J. K. (2006) They Might be Gurus, *Teacher Librarian*, **34** (1), 18–27.

Walters, D. (2007) *Hyper-Connected Generation Rises* (BBC News), http://news.bbc.co.uk/1/hi/technology/6637865.stm.

Whitmire, E. (2001) A Longitudinal Study of Undergraduates' Academic Library Experiences, *Journal of Academic Librarianship*, **27** (5), 378–85.

Williams, D. A. and Wavell, C. (2006) *Information Literacy in the Classroom: secondary school teachers' conceptions*, Robert Gordon University: Aberdeen Business School, Research Report 15.

Williams, P. (1999) Net Generation: the experiences, attitudes and behaviour of children using the Internet for their own purposes, *Aslib Proceedings*, **50** (9), 315–22.

Windham, C. (2005) Father Google and Mother IM: confessions of a NetGen learner, *Educause Review*, **40** (5), 42–59.

8

Trends in digital information consumption and the future

BARRIE GUNTER

Summary

The digital consumer society is evolving at a great pace as the communications and media landscape undergoes increasingly rapid changes. Many new information and communications technologies and linked applications are changing the way people seek out information, find entertainment and engage in civic and consumer transactions. The changes have altered the media marketplace and brought many new players into direct competition with established media operators. This has triggered exploration of new business models for the supply of information, today's primary currency across a range of commercial and social contexts. Predicting where current developments might take us is not easy. Digital consumers have more choices to make than ever before in terms of sources of information about commodities and services. They can also more readily become producers as well as consumers in the digital world with the spread of digital equipment and off-the-shelf tools that enable them to upload their own content online. The rapid evolution of new information and communications technologies has also been characterized by shrinkage in the time–lag between innovation, launch and reaching a critical mass or 'tipping point' beyond which it spreads dramatically from early adopters to the general population.

Introduction

The rapid evolution of computerized technologies and communications systems from the middle of the last decade of the 20th century has opened up a vast array of facilities and services to the public in general through which they can engage in a wide range of civic, commercial and consumer transactions. The internet has been the most prominent new communication system to emerge during this period. It provides people with access to vast quantities of information and entertainment on almost any topic imaginable and represents an important two-way communications medium for many.

In parallel to the rapid penetration of the internet, the emergence of digital technologies has wrought significant changes to longer established technologies, most notably to television and telephony, that have acquired much more diverse and interactive functionalities. In essence, the computerization of TV sets and telephony has transformed them from one-dimensional communications devices into multifunctional hubs through which a variety of forms of information can be received and sent by users. Each of these formerly distinctive technologies has acquired the defining functions of the other. Users can receive television pictures via their mobile phones, while viewers can engage in two-way communications via their digital interactive TV sets. In addition desk-top computers, when networked into the local telecommunications system, can perform all these functions and more. In essence, the growth of information systems and the significance of information as a currency have been underpinned by the accelerating rate of developments in computer technology.

The technology mergers referred to above have created an information and communications environment in which formerly distinctive communications and media activities such as publishing, broadcasting and telecommunications no longer operate in separate markets. Their overlapping functions mean that they have been brought into direct competition with each other. Television broadcasters not only face competition from other broadcasters, but also from telecommunications operators that now perceive their businesses as content providers rather than infrastructure providers. Publishers compete directly with broadcasters in many spheres of entertainment and information content provision via the internet and both must now also trade competitively against the spawn of the internet – large search engine providers that have absorbed information and entertainment content provision into their business portfolios.

The emergence of these information and communication technologies and their permeation of many aspects of every-day life have given rise to the concept of the 'information society' (Castells, 1996–8). Information has become a key trading currency in many different commercial and social contexts. Society is not simply defined by the flow of information, but also by the increasingly sophisticated electronic networks through which content can be communicated. For some writers, the adoption of new information technologies was regarded as a sign of progressiveness, whereas to avoid or reject these innovations was to be stuck in antiquity (Tapscott, 1996). The adoption of information technology innovations was also seen as a generational phenomenon. The young were separated from the old in this context and conceived of as not only acting but also thinking differently (Tapscott, 1998). As the internet and other digital technologies have developed, the idea of an 'internet generation' that is age-defined has received mixed support. Evidence discussed later in this chapter bears testimony to that observation. Even so, the digital age has changed the way many people live their lives and many organizations conduct their daily business. It has also changed the shape of many business landscapes, offering greater operational flexibility, but also bringing new sources of competition. The digital age has also introduced a new form of consumerism in which the consumer now has more choice and more power.

The recognition that digital communications markets are more competitive than those in the pre-digital era is reinforced by findings showing that use of new electronic media can displace consumption of older media. There is mounting evidence that the amount of time spent watching television, using the telephone, reading books and newspapers can be reduced by the use of the internet and related online communications networks (James, Wotring and Forrest, 1995; Robinson, Barth and Kohut, 1997; Kayany and Yelsma, 2000). Even before the internet, research found that young people who used computers a lot spent less time with newspapers, radio and television (Reagan, 1987). Thus, such displacement effects have been known to exist for some time. What is significant in the early years of the 21st century is the richness of the media and communications environment that provides digital consumers with more choice and also promotes the fragmentation of digital information markets. With the internet especially, users who go online a lot frequently report reducing their attention to other media (Wray, 2008).

One factor that drives displacement of older media by newer ones is the extent to which they have functional equivalence. Later in this chapter, we will see that the degree of shared functional equivalence between a new digital application and existing digital or pre-digital applications can mediate pace of innovation adoption. It can also influence the degree to which the use of one medium is displaced by use of a newer one. Hence, if the internet is regarded as an attractive source of entertainment, it could displace TV viewing if going online produces a higher level of gratification as a source of entertainment (Ferguson and Perse, 2000). The internet has emerged as an important communications medium, underlined in particular by the rapid adoption of online social networking applications. For some users, going online provides an effective alternative to direct, face-to-face communication (Papacharissi and Rubin, 2000). This does not mean, however, that regular internet users are or become socially isolated and depend more on virtual friends than light users or non-users. Comparisons have shown that internet users and non-users report similarly sized social networks. Internet users may actually be more socially active in that they use e-mail as an additional form of socializing and also remain relatively socially active through face-to-face contact (Franzen, 2000).

The attraction of the digital online world is that it can cater to a range of needs and interests. It has therefore not only transformed the business models of those organizations already involved in communications operations, it has also opened up new modi operandi for those working across the public and private sectors. New forms of commerce have emerged with the internet. Information and communication technology innovations are also having a major impact on the education system. People can now go online to conduct their personal banking, to pay their taxes, to book travel and holidays, and to purchase all kinds of goods from the weekly household shopping to luxury items such as household furnishings, motor vehicles and properties. They can buy and sell through online auction sites. They can obtain personal advice about health, jobs and careers, legal matters and personal life plans. They can track family histories, locate old friends and find new companions. They can also present their daily diaries online and share their day-to-day experiences with friends and strangers. The rapid adoption of digital technologies has enabled many people to create virtual or 'digital' lives for themselves that run in parallel with the ordinary, offline lives. Information is the primary currency in this digital world and its users are all digital information consumers and creators.

The world has changed so rapidly within just a few years and the pace of that change is not only continuing but accelerating. The idea that new information and communications technology developments are the preserve of the young is also dissolving with evidence that all generations have become digital adopters in one way or another (Ofcom, 2007a). The younger generation may have dominated the early adopters of the internet and various fixed and mobile digital interactive technologies (Blair, 2004; Tapscott, 1998), but within the late majority of adopters, the grey market (i.e. people aged over 50) is significantly represented (Madden, 2005; Ofcom, 2007a).

Certainly, the young dominated early adoption of the internet per se, but each successive older generation has displayed 'catch-up', lagging around three years behind their children. Hence, reported internet use by the young in the United States grew from 83% in 2000 to a near universal 98% by 2003. Adults old enough to be the parents of the latter generation, aged 36–45 years, displayed reported growth in internet use from 69% to 87% over the same period. Hence, their position in 2003 matched that of 12–15-year-olds in 2000. Moving up another generation to those adults aged 56–65 years, reported internet use grew from 55% in 2000 to 67% in 2003. Once again, the 2003 position for the older generation matched the 2000 position for the next generation down (Cole et al., 2004).

Although the 'digital divide' associated with age has diminished in regard to internet connectivity and the use of some online applications, elsewhere it has been reported to persist. Significant age-related differences still exist in the UK in relation to use of online social networking sites. While over half of 15–19-year-old males claimed to be regular browsers of these sites, only a small minority (13%) of 45–54-year-old males made the same claim (Wray, 2008).

The difficulty of making predictions

The earlier chapters in this book have indicated that the digital world is a rapidly changing one. It is important for scholars in the academy and practitioners operating across a range of public and commercial systems to understand not only the potential of digital technologies but also the abilities of digital consumers to cope with the new opportunities opened up by digital innovations. Digital systems must work properly and have relevance to digital consumers. They must be user friendly and also often observe or at least be aware of the normal rules and conventions of human communication.

Predicting the future is far from straightforward. Future forecasts tend to be based on historical trends. In a world that is evolving at varying rates, old innovation adoption trends may not always provide accurate predictive models. Even if we utilize rates of adoption of 'old' technologies – print publishing in its different forms, radio and television broadcasting, home video-recorders or early computer games – these may not yield accurate predictive models from which we can gauge how quickly new digital information platforms and associated applications will spread.

Changing economic, political, social and cultural circumstances within which innovations appear may affect adoption rates for new digital information applications (Norris, 2001). In addition, whereas innovations in the past have often represented radical departures from any previously available technologies (e.g. the adoption of computer games and home video recorders), today's much richer and more diverse communications environment tends to spin off more new applications that become established more quickly because they represent enhanced functions to existing information and communication systems (e.g. Web 2.0 applications).

Innovations can rapidly shift from being a minority interest to majority adoption once they have reached a critical mass in terms of how many users they have accumulated, a stage frequently referred to as a 'tipping point'. Past research has indicated that the critical mass, expressed in terms of the proportion of all potential users within a given population who have adopted an innovation, tends to occur somewhere between 10 and 25% penetration. As we look back over time, however, it becomes apparent just how the speed with which a tipping point is reached has changed. It took five decades for telephone technology to reach that level of penetration in the early part of the 20th century and just five years for the world wide web to do the same at the end of the same century (Chen and Crowston, 1997).

The rate of adoption is linked to whether an innovation truly is 'new' in every way or whether it represents a new version of an older model. Although the world wide web was a new phenomenon for many people, some relevant groundwork had been laid down in that growing numbers of people had learned to use computers in their workplace as well as at home (usually for playing games) by the early 1990s when the software protocols for the web were being rolled out. Moreover, an internet system that could be used to convey e-mails had been in use for many years before then by the academy and the military in the United States. Growing numbers of companies in the western world at this time were also establishing intranets – internal electronic messaging systems operating via computer stations restricted to the workforce. In the domestic sphere (e.g. at home) the penetration of computer games meant that many people had acquired relevant computer literacy skills by the time the internet started to become publicly available (Greenfield, 1984; Gunter, 1998). Once the public internet was being rolled out, therefore, significant numbers of people in developed countries had already acquired some relevant technology experience.

One relevant distinction, that helps to model innovation adoption within a rapidly changing digital information environment, is whether a new technology has no precedent or is simply a new application tagged on to an established platform or system (Liebenau, 2007). A 'transformative' innovation is an original technology unlike any before it. This requires users to go on a voyage of discovery in learning how to use it and how to take best advantage of it. In addition, there are many 'general purpose' innovations that comprise technologies with which many or most people may be familiar that continually undergo change. In these cases, new models may be produced that represent enhancements of earlier versions. Some new learning may be required on the part of their users, but the essential features and application protocols remain the same.

Taking this distinction we can ask whether Web 2.0 developments represent 'transformative' or 'general purpose' innovations. In most instances they can probably be considered exemplars of the latter rather than the former. What slightly confuses the issue is that the earlier versions upon which Web 2.0 applications are based have also had a short and changeable life span. In some cases, new upgrades occur even before the older models have reached a tipping point among the wider population.

Despite the debate about whether they represent genuinely new or transformative innovations, there is little doubt that the growth of the internet and world wide web has been astounding. The first web server was introduced in 1991 and five years later there were almost a quarter of a million of them in different parts of the world. That growth has continued unabated as have the number and range of related applications (Liebenau, 2007). Even knowing that transformative and general purpose distinctions can provide a rough guide to the likelihood of rapid as opposed to only fairly rapid penetration of digital innovations, forecasting the future still remains imprecise because the saturation of markets with functionally similar applications could also drive varying rates of adoption. Furthermore, if a new application is functionally very similar to an existing one, will it add to penetration of that class of innovations or it will simply cannibalize existing competitors without necessarily leading to overall market size growth (i.e. motivate non-adopters to adopt)?

The significance of digital technology convergence

Transformative and general purpose innovations represent distinct categories of digital development that can lead to different predictions about rates of innovation adoption. What can further complicate predictions about future digital market growth is the phenomenon of technology convergence. It has already been noted that formerly distinct sectors such as publishing, broadcasting, telecommunications, to which we can also add computer hardware and software manufacturers, and internet search engines now operate increasingly within the same marketplaces. One of the key drivers behind this trend has been technology convergence. This phenomenon is primarily manifested in the increasingly computerized functionality of telephone and television technologies. It is also seen in the technical enhancements and increased functionality of computer games consoles.

Television programmes can now be received over two other platforms – the internet and mobile phones – in addition to over standard TV sets. Newspapers can be read online as well as from print copies. Standalone computer games consoles can now provide online hubs through which a wide range of content can be received and manipulated. Mobile phones can be used to upload picture and text content onto the internet.

These changes have been reflected in turn in new business partnerships between service suppliers that were once associated with distinct sectors of provision with their own non-overlapping markets of operation. Thus, BSkyB, a broadcaster, and Google, a search engine, teamed up to provide web-based search, advertising and video services to broadband internet subscribers. Vodafone, a telecommunications operator, and Google have jointly produced a portfolio of internet-based services available via mobile phones. The BBC and YouTube, a social network provider, have teamed up to supply BBC-branded entertainment channels to the social network's subscriber base. BT, a telecommunications operator, has joined with Sony (Japan), a computer and electronics manufacturer, to add wireless broadband internet functionality to computer games consoles allowing such devices to be used for voice calls, video and text messaging as well as game playing (see Ofcom, 2007b).

The significance of these developments for information searching and educational applications derives from the implications they have for seamlessly switching between technologies for a range of different applications provided in different modalities. Such developments could cultivate a different mindset on the part of future generations in respect of the application expectations of specific technologies and will increase the choices of information consumers in terms of opportunities to obtain, use, and create content and in the tools that will become available to communicate content with others.

New functions created for specific communications technologies can help to maintain their market position in increasingly competitive markets. However, to enhance the attractiveness of a digital technology, enhanced functionality needs to meet consumer needs, represent a good fit as an application to the technology, be easy to use and be provided at a cost that consumers are prepared to tolerate. The increasingly varied use of mobile phones is perhaps one of the best examples of these developments. These are no longer purely voice messaging devices. Mobile phones are today widely used for sending text messages, creating and storing picture files, accessing the internet, and reception of music, speech broadcasts and television programmes (Ofcom, 2007b).

Will digital consumers change?

Regardless of whether we can accurately predict the future shape of digital information consumption, one thing seems fairly certain and that is that there has been and is likely to continue to be an expansion of the amount of digital content being made available to digital consumers. Does this evolving information environment also mean that digital consumers will also have to evolve along with it? Will digital consumers have to learn new strategies for engaging with this burgeoning information environment? Will they have to acquire new competencies to deal with increased amounts and varieties of information? Is there any evidence that such changes are occurring and, if so, are they universal or restricted mostly to particular market segments? Is there a generational divide, for example, in online literacy?

We know that there has been a dramatic growth in digital technologies and information systems since the mid-1990s. Is there any evidence for the emergence of a 'digital generation' that has only really known the digital era and that therefore uses digital innovations differently from pre-digital generations? Some writers have argued that those brought up in the internet era differ from the television generation not least because of the distinctive cognitive orientations required by each technology (Tapscott, 1998). The 'net' is an active medium that requires users to seek out content and engage with it in a psychologically dynamic way. Television, in contrast, is a passive medium that encourages or invites viewers to sit back and allow its content to wash over them. It has been argued that television viewers are more often happy to settle for what they are given. Internet surfers are continually on the lookout for new experiences and seek more opportunities to satisfy their curiosity. As such the 'net' generation acquires a new form of literacy and for them using online technology comes naturally (Tapscott, 1998).

This viewpoint has not been universally accepted. For other observers of new media developments, a technology-deterministic perspective fails to recognize that technology innovations are never established in a complete vacuum, but occur within political, economic, social and cultural contexts that affect the extent to which they are adopted and the way they are adopted (Webster, 1995). It is certainly the case that digital divides exist, but these are linked to political, economic and cultural circumstances and these factors can go some way towards explaining different rates of internet adoption between different countries and between different sub-groups of populations within countries (Norris, 2001).

New technologies can be regarded as providing fresh opportunities for younger generations to learn and experience the world. These opportunities carry various potential benefits and risks to young people. They can only effectively be understood, however, when considered in the context of the surrounding political, economic, social and cultural milieu in which technology innovations occur (Buckingham, 2000, 2005).

As to whether digital consumers evolve as consumers or as human information processors as a function of their experiences with interactive media such as the internet, is a point on which there has been much debate. Clearly, the internet on the surface looks different from older media such as books, magazines, newspapers and television. However, it also contains all the types of content that the latter media convey. The mere presence of the internet and the fact that growing numbers of people use it may not be sufficient to produce qualitative changes in the way people think about, use and search for information or engage in communication transactions with other people.

In the case of children – the youngest users of technology innovations and often the quickest to try them out – a great deal of online behaviour is fairly mundane. They turn to the internet to e-mail or chat to their friends, download music, and visit websites run by, on behalf of, or about, celebrity icons. Online technologies have provided new ways for them to keep in touch with their social network and to find information about subjects they would have probably been seeking anyway through other available means in the absence of the internet. Internet behaviour is generally not dramatically innovative and different in the context of information search and use (Holloway and Valentine, 2003).

Digital information consumers or 'prosumers'?

Despite the debates about whether engagement with digital information technologies is creating a new generation of digital information consumers who think and behave differently from pre-digital generations, there can be no dispute about the fact that the internet has opened up multiple new sources of content and forms of interactive communication. One of the most significant developments that has characterized and is often taken to define the second web generation is the availability of tools through which digital information consumers can also become digital information producers. Rather than being simply consumers, they are now also 'prosumers'.

The internet has not only provided a channel through which users can download content but also upload it. Off-the-shelf tools and online service providers have enabled online consumers to become producers. Growing numbers of internet users maintain their own websites increasingly in the form of online diaries – weblogs or 'blogs' – which they regularly update with information about themselves or topics of interest. The impact of blogs, however, is limited given that most of these sites receive few visitors (Deloitte, 2007a).

Communities of internet users have contrived to create vast online information repositories that are maintained and updated by the people who consume them. Wikipedia has emerged as probably the biggest and best known repository of this type and is available in over 250 languages

(Ofcom, 2007b). In addition, a multitude of online social networks has emerged in which individuals produce and post content about themselves and establish links with others who do likewise. These networks have social functions in that they represent environments in which individuals can maintain contact with people they already know as well as making new social (and business) contacts. Such networks can also serve as information exchanges where online social contacts can provide advice, opinions, recommendations and critiques on a wide range of issues. Online social networks have been widely adopted, especially by young people in the 15–30 age bracket (Deloitte, 2007a).

A great deal of user-generated content is created and shared on social networking sites. While much of the messaging that takes place comprises textual content, the sharing of video content has been made extremely popular by sites such as YouTube. The fact of online users becoming video producers as well as regular consumers of such home-made material raises questions about whether this has important implications for established television broadcasters. So far, the volume of video viewing via YouTube does not pose a direct threat to the markets for television companies because the average YouTube video is only a few minutes long and average viewing durations tend to be quite short. So despite figures showing that YouTube fields 100 million downloads a day and attracts 70 million unique users per month, the total volume of worldwide viewing of online videos via this network adds up to only one-tenth of the amount of viewing of the BBC in the UK alone (Deloitte, 2007a). The displacement effects of one medium upon another that have been observed to occur with the introduction and uptake of new online media (e.g. Kayany and Yelsma, 2000), however, suggest that as these social networking sites attract more 'prosumers' it is inevitable that they will occupy more of people's time and that time budget allocations to other media will be adjusted as a result.

Finding the tipping point

We have already seen that one key variable in deciding whether a digital technology innovation is likely to be a major force in the future is whether the technology, or a new application of it, has reached a critical mass of adoption beyond which further rapid penetration will follow. Historical analyses of adoption of innovations have indicated that this point is usually reached at between 10% and 25% penetration of the potential user population.

On this basis, it is clear that certain internet applications have become established, others are on their way to becoming so, while still others have some way to go. In countries such as the USA and UK, the internet reached a 'tipping point' among most age groups by 2000. Other countries in the developed world displayed similar levels of penetration and adoption by 2005. In mature internet markets, it is only the over 65-year-olds that lag behind in general internet adoption.

The internet, however, is the base technology for many different applications. Moreover, as a technology, the initial internet was founded upon standard telephone networks that offered limited information transmission capacity. The emergence of broadband changed all that. The broadband internet can accommodate large quantities of data in different formats. It has proven to be essential for more advanced online transactions that involve very large files of data. Hence, broadband penetration has been a key development underpinning the rapid growth of Web 2.0 applications. The tipping point for broadband has occurred much more recently in developed online markets. By 2006, four in ten people in the UK (39%) reportedly had a broadband internet connection (Ofcom, 2006). The level of broadband adoption was widespread among all age groups up to 65, but was most widely adopted among those aged 15–24 years (81% of internet users in that age group).

Web 2.0 is an umbrella term that embraces a range of online applications innovations, rather than hard technology developments, that have occurred primarily since 2000. These developments reflect the increasingly widespread use of the internet for content creation and social networking. These applications have so far been used mostly for personal and social reasons, but they also provide tools that are already demonstrating value in other settings such as consumer information exchange and the performance of commercial organizations and services. To what extent though have these innovations reached their own tipping points?

A lot of attention has been attracted by blogging. While weblogs or 'blogs' represent personal diaries that are regularly updated in relation to almost any subject, their profile has been raised most significantly by journalism blogs that have become established as alternative news sources. The earliest recorded blog of this sort occurred in 1998 in relation to a southern US newspaper's coverage of a major hurricane (Singer, 2003, 2005). It was during the aftermath of the event of 9/11 that news blogging really took off (see Allan, 2006). The significance of this form of online journalism was further reinforced during the November 2004 US Presidential election campaign which saw an explosion of both news blogs and political blogs (Lawson-Borders and Kirk, 2005).

The penetration figures for blogging, however, show that it is on the cusp of reaching a critical mass in some markets and not others. Evidence for the UK showed that just one in six internet users in general (16%) claimed to have contributed to a blog, although this claim was much more prevalent among those aged 16–24 years (37%) (Ofcom, 2006). In another survey conducted only with internet users aged 16–24 years, only around one in ten (11%) said they had ever blogged (Synovate, 2007).

In the US, only 9% of internet users said they had ever created a blog (Lenhart, 2007). Given that two-thirds of Americans were online at this time this represents 6% of the general population. Blog creation was more than twice as widespread among 12–17-year-olds (19%) and 18–28-year-olds (20%). As 87% and 84% of these two age groups reportedly went online at this time, this meant that in 2005 17% of all (offline and online) individuals across these age groups had created a blog. Blog creation was also more widespread among internet users with broadband connections (11% compared to 4% dial-up connections). Blog use remains on the cusp of the tipping point zone in the UK, while blog creation has not reached that zone yet. In the US, blog creation has reached the tipping point zone among those aged under 29, but not yet among older people.

Another online information source to which users can contribute as content providers is Wikipedia. American research among internet users found that significant minorities reported using this source, but usage gradually declines with age (Rainie and Tancer, 2007). The biggest users were those aged 18–29 (44%), followed by those aged 30–49 (38%). College graduates were also more likely than others to be users (50%). In this case, however, two kinds of use – as a reference source or as a contributor – were not distinguished. In an e-learning context, both types of utility are anticipated for wiki technology. Nonetheless, these findings indicate that wikis are being widely used by young people and a tipping point has been passed among many age groups.

Social networking sites have been identified as another Web 2.0 leisure activity that could have more valuable applications in a formal learning context. In research conducted across Europe with internet users, nearly one in four (23%) said they used an online social network at least once a month, a figure that grew to nearly one in three (32%) among 16–24-year-olds (European Interactive Advertising Association, 2007). In the US, while only a minority of the general population (16%) said they used online social networking sites, this figure grew dramatically to over half (55%) of 12–17-year-olds (Lenhart, 2007; Lenhart, Madden and Hitlin, 2005). Since, by 2000, most teenagers in the US admitted to using e-mail and instant messaging with friends in the context of school assignments, the latest social networking phenomenon may enable them to widen the net of social contacts who might also be used as an education support group.

Finding the right functionality

Recent predictions for the telecommunications and media worlds by one major consultancy have pointed out that while technology infrastructures have been established to ensure that most people in developed countries potentially can gain access to basic applications, connectivity *per se* does not remove all digital divides (Deloitte, 2007a, 2007b). In the case of the internet, for example, there are varying degrees of connectivity. To take full advantage of advanced applications of the online world, broadband connectivity is essential. Yet, this technology has not reached, or been adopted by, everyone. Even where governments have taken steps to facilitate broadband penetration, a plateau can be reached quite quickly with significant proportions of the population remaining without connectivity. In the United States, broadband penetration reached 60% in 2002, but by 2006 it had only grown to 70%. In the United Kingdom, nearly one in ten internet users surveyed were lapsed users. Meanwhile, among non-users, a clear majority indicated that they had no intention of acquiring an internet connection in the next year.

One of the key problems holding back universal or near-universal penetration could be the centrality of the personal computer to accessing the internet. The PC alone, however, does not make the internet relevant for everyone. For some applications, such as video-conferencing, additional equipment must be obtained to enhance the functionality of the basic PC. The most popular online activities comprise e-mail, search, surfing, shopping, booking travel, messaging, listening to and downloading music, and playing games. Some of these activities are best handled by the PC with its full keyboard. Others could be effectively handled by other devices. E-mail and messaging, for example, could be appropriately handled by mobile devices (Deloitte, 2007b).

In considering what might happen in the future, therefore, the digital technology adoption patterns indicate that digital information consumers are displaying normative use of Web 2.0 technologies across a range of information gathering and consumer transaction contexts. This observation is especially true of younger digital information consumers, but is increasingly becoming the case with a growing number of applications even among older consumers. Each older generation is catching up with the next younger generation down, and lags just three to four years behind in terms of full membership of the digital information society. New online applications are being developed at a growing pace and the time lag from innovation to tipping point for many new applications is shrinking.

References

Allan, S. (2006) *Online News*, Open University Press.
Blair, A. (2004) *Playstation Generation could be Alone for Life*,
    www.timesonline.co.uk/article/0,7947-1335635,00.html.

Buckingham, D. (2000) *After the Death of Childhood: growing up in the age of electronic media*, Cambridge, Polity.

Buckingham, D. (2005) Children and New Media. In Lievrouw, L. and Livingstone, S. (eds), *Handbook of New Media*, 2nd edn, Sage, 75–91.

Castells, M. (1996–1998) *The Information Age*, Vols I–III, Blackwell.

Chen, H. G. and Crowston, K. (1997) Comparative Diffusion of the Telephone and World Wide Web: an analysis of rates of adoption, www.crowston.syr.edu/papers/webnet97 [accessed 4 June 2007].

Cole, J. I., Suman, M., Schramm, P., Lunn, R. and Aquino, J. S. (2004) *Ten Years, Ten Trends: the digital future report – surveying the digital future, Year 4.* USC Annenberg School, Center for the Digital Future, Los Angeles.

Deloitte (2007a) *Media Predictions: TMT Trends 2007*, www.deloitte.com/dtt/cda/doc/content/dtt_mediaPredictions011107.

Deloitte (2007b) *Telecommunications Predictions: TMT Trends 2007*, www.usiia.org/news/dtt_TelecomPredictions.

European Interactive Advertising Association (2007) *Social Networking to Drive Next Wave of Internet Usage*, www.eiaa.net/news/eiaa-articles-details.asp?id=1068.

Ferguson, D. and Perse, E. (2000) The World Wide Web as a Functional Alternative to Television, *Journal of Broadcasting and Electronic Media*, **44** (2), 155–74.

Franzen, A. (2000) Does the Internet Make us Lonely?, *European Sociological Review*, **16** (4), 427–38.

Greenfield, P. M. (1984) *Mind and Media: the effects of television, computers and video games*, Fontana.

Gunter, B. (1998) *The Effects of Video Games on Children: the myth unmasked*, University of Sheffield Press.

Holloway, S. and Valentine, G. (2003) *Cyberkids: children in the information age*, Routledge.

James, M., Wotring, C. and Forrest, E. (1995) An Exploratory Study of the Perceived Benefits of Electronic Bulletin Board Use and Their Impact on Other Communication Activities, *Journal of Broadcasting and Electronic Media*, **39**, 30–50.

Kayany, J. and Yelsma, P. (2000) Displacement Effects of Online Media in the Socio-Technical Contexts of Households, *Journal of Broadcasting and Electronic Media*, **44** (2), 215–29.

Lawson-Borders, G. and Kirk, R. (2005) Blogs in Campaign Communication, *American Behavioral Scientist,* **49** (4), 548–59.

Lenhart, A. (2007) *Social Networking Websites and Teens: an overview*, Pew Internet and American Life Project, www.pewinternet.org.

Lenhart, A., Madden, M. and Hitlin, P. (2005) *Teens and Technology*, Pew Internet and American Life Project, Washington, DC, www.pewinternet.org.

Liebenau, J. (2007) *Innovation Trends: prioritising emerging technologies shaping the UK to 2017*, DTI Occasional Paper, No. 8, Department of Trade and Industry.

Madden, M. (2005) *Generations Online*, Pew Internet and American Life Project, Washington, DC, December, www.pewinternet.org.

Norris, P. (2001) *Digital Divide: civic engagement, information poverty and the internet worldwide*, New York, NY, Cambridge University Press.

Ofcom (2006, November) *The Consumer Experience*, London, Office for Communications.

Ofcom (2007a) *Communications Market Report: converging communications markets*, Research Document, London, Office for Communications.

Ofcom (2007b) *The International Communications Market 2007*, Research Document, London, Office for Communications.

Papacharissi, Z. and Rubin, A. (2000) Predictors of Internet Use, *Journal of Broadcasting and Electronic Media*, **44** (2), 175–96.

Rainie, L. and Tancer, B. (2007) *Data Memo: 36% of online American adults consult Wikipedia*, Pew Internet and American Life Project, www.pewinternet.org.

Reagan, J. (1987) Classifying Adopters and Non-Adopters of Four Technologies Using Political Activity, Media Use and Demographic Variables, *Telematics and Informatics*, **4**, 3–16.

Robinson, J., Barth, K. and Kohut, A. (1997) Social Impact Research: personal computers, mass media and use of time, *Social Science Computer Review*, **15** (1), 65–82.

Singer, J. B. (2003) Who are these Guys?: the online challenge to the notion of journalistic professionalism, *Journalism*, **4** (2), 139–63.

Singer, J. B. (2005) The Political J-Blogger: 'Normalizing' a New Media Form to Fit Old Norms and Practices, *Journalism*, **6** (2), 172–98.

Synovate (2007) *Leisure Time: clean living youth shun new technology*, www.synovate.com/current/news/article/2007/02.

Tapscott, D. (1996) *The Digital Economy: promise and peril in an age of networked intelligence*, McGraw-Hill.

Tapscott, D. (1998) *Growing up Digital: the rise of the net generation*, McGraw-Hill.

Webster, F. (1995) *Theories of the Information Society*, Routledge.

Wray, R. (2008) Digital Kids Ditch Homework for Networking, *The Guardian*, 3 March, 25.

9

Where do we go from here?

DAVID NICHOLAS

The book has comprehensively examined the digital space and its consumers, from all disciplines and angles. It has been undertaken from historical and futuristic perspectives. We have identified the problems and challenges in a direct and earthy manner, and have sometimes been hard on the information professions, and rightly so given the perilous situation they find themselves in. But where, if anywhere, do we go from here? What can be done on a practical basis to ensure, for instance, that consumers consume more in 'our' information space and do not continue to fly into the arms of others, or, indeed, do it all themselves? All the book's contributors were asked to provide one suggestion and readers will be pleased to learn that nobody said 'the last one out turn the lights off', although a few were close to saying this. Also, the fact that this is the shortest chapter, by a long way, should send out the important message that there are not that many ways out of the current situation – between a rock (Google) and a hard place (the e-shopper). On the other hand, with so few solutions on offer they should be easy to remember and, hopefully, easier to achieve, especially as they require very little in the way of resource. In most cases, they simply require a new mindset. The suggestions offered follow in order of priority:

1   **Live with the prospect of constant change.** As consumers are the drivers of change, this entails getting very close to the digital consumer (especially the younger ones) and remaining close – connecting in other words. This is a continuous, ongoing and mainstream process, and should not be undertaken just when there is time or a problem. A great start can be made by monitoring digital transactions (the logs) and following up the questions raised in questionnaire and interview. Establish user monitoring units, experiment and introduce change; do not let your services become stuck in digital concrete. As far as we are aware, no one has yet done this.

2   **Establish a link with information provision and access/outcomes.** Demonstrate that the professional information investment delivers benefits or outcomes (e.g. health, scholarly). Access is not an outcome in itself.

3   **Keep it simple.** A counsel of despair, quite probably, but one of the conclusions of the Google Generation project was that virtual library spaces are very complex and need simplifying. Interfaces need to be involving and the problem these days is that digital consumers increasingly benchmark their online experiences against more immersive environments like Amazon or Facebook. One of the leitmotivs of our whole experience of the virtual scholar is that convenience and user satisfaction will triumph, even over content, any day of the week. Why can't library catalogues be like Amazon with sample pages, trust metrics, referral metrics, user feedback and *colour*? Why do they not speak to the user? Look around at your environment, it is much bigger and more different than you think (just ask the user). Have you ever considered what other close occupants of the virtual space call themselves – Facebook, Bebo, BBCi, Google, and Yahoo? Why not blend in, join the community – why stand out like a sore thumb? Too many sites produced by information professionals and publishers are monastic.

4   **Do not be seduced by digital fashions, they will all disappear.** Deal in what you know works now. Do not become sidetracked by institutional repositories, portals, internet cafes, open access and social

networks as you will not find salvation there; salvation instead lies with better understanding the digital consumer, and returning to old strengths like collection management. In this regard wake up to the fact that e-books will be the next really big challenge. The seismic shift that will unquestionably happen will fundamentally change the information space (in fact, decrease the physical space) and will grow and change the population of digital consumers significantly.

5   **Get social.** Forget all notions of broadcast one-to-many publishing/information access and build conversations with audience. Also cooperate with other players, especially commercial services. They are good examples: OCLC cooperating with Google, Yahoo, and Amazon, many libraries cooperating on the Google Scholar mass digitization project. The digital visibility provided by the likes of Google for traditional information services is enormous. Call it digital piggy-backing if you like, but it works. Share the spoils, do not fight over them. Our fight is not with Google, it is with ourselves.

6   **Hold on to the physical space.** A solution that is trotted out by many beleaguered information professionals is the library as a physical gathering/studying/reflective space. This, of course, is roots stuff. We think the jury is out on this one. In one sense the idea is not new enough, big enough; nor does it chime with the evidence. If e-textbooks become a reality, as we expect, this should create plenty of space, but of course this will become teaching and learning space, something which academic staff have a big interest in. Also with wireless networks the whole campus, town, train, coffee shop becomes a learning and teaching space – which space, then, is preferred, more convenient? We know for sure that young (and old) people increasingly love the virtual space. In another sense this is an area where information professionals have no competition and there are clearly some cultural and scholarly benefits here.

Build that dialogue with the consumer, never forget they have *choice*, remember that we are all part of a much bigger information universe now and follow and adapt to the behaviour of the e-shopper. Finally, the information community must stop thinking it knows best, otherwise it will be in danger of becoming irrelevant. The consumer knows best.

Index